W^c
LIGHT

Spiritual Wisdom from the

Dead Sea Scrolls

KENNETH HANSON, PH.D.

COUNCIL OAK BOOKS
SAN FRANCISCO/TULSA

Council Oak Books, LLC
1290 Chestnut Street, Suite 2
San Francisco, CA 94109
1350 E. 15th Street, Tulsa, OK 74120
WORDS OF LIGHT: *Spiritual Wisdom*
from the Dead Sea Scrolls.

Library of Congress Cataloging-in-Publication Data
Hanson, Kenneth, 1953–
    Words of light : spiritual wisdon from the Dead
    Sea scrolls / Kenneth Hanson.—1st ed.
        p. cm.
    Includes bibliographical references.
    ISBN 1-57178-090-4
    1. Essenes. 2. Dead Sea scrolls—Criticism, inter-
    pretation, etc. I. Title.
    BM 175.E8 H35 2000
    296.1'55—dc21   99-089126
First edition / First printing.
Printed in Canada
00 01 02 03 04 05 06   5 4 3 2 1

CONTENTS

Introduction

THE YOUNG MAN CLUTCHED HIS NEW PASSPORT IN HIS HAND
and marched toward the jetway. He waved to his teary-eyed
parents and an ad hoc assemblage of friends—old high school
buddies in the main—and slowly disappeared down the long
corridor leading from the O'Hare Airport International
Terminal, directly into the belly of a McDonell-Douglas DC-10.

It was the last day of December 1977, and this boyish-
looking college student, a senior at the University of Illinois at
Chicago, was walking onto an airplane for only the second
time in his life. The thrill of flight alone would have been
enough to excite him, but the destination of this jumbo jet—
Zurich, Switzerland—left him with a mixture of speechless awe
and nervous apprehension. Nine grueling hours after takeoff,
his face pressed to the glass all the way, he landed in the heart
of Europe at Zurich International Airport, where he would
change planes. His adrenaline rush not having allowed him a
wink of sleep, he stumbled his way to the most heavily guarded
gate of the airport—destination: Tel Aviv. There, in front of
him, stood an incredible array of characters: a menagerie of
men and women, clutching their suitcases and their children.
There were ultraorthodox Hasidim with their black coats and
long side curls, assorted olive-skinned Israeli families bantering

in Hebrew, and Palestinians, some wearing *kafias* on their heads, busily chattering in Arabic.

Israeli security people were greatly in evidence, tearing open luggage and inspecting the contents, piece by piece. Next, they carefully scrutinized each passport, proffering a bureaucratic nod. The slender young man flashed his own passport, bearing a special student visa, affording him "permanent residence" status in the state of Israel. With the passage of another six hours, the second DC-10 he boarded thudded upon the runway at Tel Aviv's Ben Gurion Airport, to the accompaniment of sincere applause from the passengers, home again in their ancient land.

Alighting upon the tarmac was for him the most exhilarating experience of his life. But ahead lay Passport Control and more security checks. After what seemed an endless wait, the young sojourner retrieved his one piece of luggage—an enormous green duffel bag he had procured during his service in the U.S. Army—and boarded a bus bound for the city of Jerusalem.

I scarcely remember that young man—myself—all alone, on my life's first journey outside the continental United States. The culture shock was immediate and harsh. I was not a tourist on holiday. I had come to the Middle East to live, to sink some roots, at least for the foreseeable future, to embark on a long and difficult path, of both undergraduate and graduate study. At the moment, however, my knowledge was meager. I understood not a word of the language, had difficulties with the currency, and was utterly bewildered by the array of Middle Eastern cuisine I would soon encounter. As the bus lurched its way along the winding and circuitous route from Tel Aviv to Jerusalem, up the steeply inclining Judean hillsides, the radio blared an assortment of Middle Eastern melodies, combined with Israeli pop-rock in Hebrew. What a curious experience, to hear the ancient tongue of the prophets intoned to the accompaniment of electric guitar, bass, and a pounding drumbeat.

Half an hour later, a second city bus deposited me at Jaffa Gate, the main entrance to the Old City of Jerusalem. It was like gazing on antiquity itself. The grayish limestone walls, built by the Turkish sultan Suleiman the Magnificent and topped by Muslim minarets, towered in front of me. Inside the Old City walls, I continued along a narrow asphalt road leading to my ultimate destination—Mount Zion.

I soon found myself standing before an ashen stone gate that marked the entrance to Mount Zion's American Institute for Holy Land Studies. There, I was greeted by other Americans, who showed me to my quarters deep inside a structure built in the previous century and formerly used by the British to house a school of their own. There was no heating system, and in Jerusalem's January cold, the only recourse was to light small kerosene burners, huddling close enough for warmth but far enough away to avoid inhaling the noxious fumes.

It wasn't long before I began toying with the idea of packing up and going home. But in the end I gritted my teeth, adopted as spartan an attitude as I could, and steeled my soul for the adventure that lay ahead. Within a couple of days after my arrival, classes began and I was immersed in the study of the ancient Near East—the entire biblical world, its culture, language, and archaeology. As a young historian, I came to understand how the three great cultures of the modern world—Judaism, Christianity, and Islam—are directly rooted in common soil. I would perceive the intrinsic unity of these cultures, and the forces in history that caused them to diverge.

I would also encounter, through my studies, a curious group of ancient Judeans. They were never very large numerically, and they would probably have remained unknown to us, were it not for the fact that during the two centuries of their existence, precisely two millennia ago, they transcribed a veritable library of documents. These included copies of the Hebrew scriptures (the Bible); their own rule books and manuals; assorted psalms and liturgical documents; and mystical visions of the divine realm, the end of the age, and eschatological conflict between the forces of good and evil.

They lived by the principles of a strict covenant between themselves and the Almighty. They referred to themselves most often as the "Sons of Light." An ancient Jewish historian of the first century, Josephus Flavius, referred to this same group by another name. He called them the "Essenes," a term that today has become closely identified with what we have come to call the Dead Sea Scrolls.

These ancient Sons of Light not only transcribed this small library of Hebrew texts, they systematically interred them in a series of caves—some natural and some that they dug into the limestone cliffs that rim the western shore of the lowest spot on the face of the earth, the Dead Sea. For some unknown reason about which we can only speculate, this brave little sect of ancient Judeans disappeared in the late first century of the Common Era. Their lives and their legacy, aside from the brief descriptive passages by the historian Josephus, would have been obliterated forever were it not for the fact that in 1947, a young Bedouin shepherd stumbled upon one of the caves in which these ancient parchments had been hidden. While the discovery went largely unhailed at first, over time it gave birth to a frenzied rush, on the part of archaeologists and Bedouin alike, to comb every cave, every nook and cranny up and down the western shore of the Dead Sea, to see just how much priceless parchment material could be retrieved.

The results were far beyond anyone's expectations. Today the corpus of the Dead Sea Scrolls, divided between West Jerusalem's Shrine of the Book museum (an annex of the Israel Museum of Jerusalem) and the East Jerusalem Rockefeller Museum, represents the most important manuscript find of the twentieth century, perhaps the most important ever.

For me, as a young history student in Jerusalem who spoke not a word of Hebrew, their contents remained shrouded in mystery. Determined to divest myself of every trace of culture shock, I enrolled, upon completion of my semester of study at the American Institute, in a language course for new immigrants to the state of Israel. The more I learned, the more intoxicated I became with the idea that I might not only read and write this modern yet ancient language, but that I could live it, breathe it, sleep it, dream it.

After a few months of study, I decided to test myself one afternoon by hopping on a Jerusalem city bus bound for the Shrine of the Book. The shrine is a great rotunda, built of poured, sculpted concrete. An enormous dome, in the shape of the lid of one of the ancient jars in which the Dead Sea Scrolls were found, shoots up overhead. In the holy hush of that dimly lit sanctuary, I first confronted the Dead Sea Scrolls "up close and personal." While I had already studied about them, I was now able to read them, for Hebrew as a language has remained virtually unchanged for the last two millennia or more. That afternoon I decided to pursue my study of the Dead Sea Scrolls, ultimately toward a doctorate degree in Hebrew language and literature.

For the immediate future, I contented myself with becoming fluent in my new language. My humble accommodations—the little room behind the pediatrician's office—afforded me an excellent opportunity to experience personally the things I was studying. Like the ancient Essenes, I was learning a simple, spartan life, uncluttered and uncomplicated. I was learning to understand the principles that drove these ancient Judeans into the desert to begin with. In the afternoons, I cooked pots of stew on a small gas burner. By night I slept on a little cot on the floor. I woke each day with the light of dawn. Simplicity ruled. In those days in Israel, air-conditioning in private dwellings was uncommon. So, to cool off I would take long strolls in the evening, from West Jerusalem into East Jerusalem, and beyond. I would trudge my way up the Mount of Olives in order to gain a grand panorama of the city by night. I stood where saints and prophets had walked, from time immemorial, simply to take it all in.

There in the distance the moonlight brightened the golden cupola known as the Dome of the Rock, a mosque that sits majestically upon the site of the ancient temple of Solomon. Somewhat beyond the golden dome was the blackish dome of the Church of the Holy Sepulchre, where long ago Jesus of Nazareth was both crucified and entombed. Here, three great world religions, three cultures, come together in a single city, Jerusalem, whose very name means "peace," but which has never known it.

Today, after twenty years of reflection and fifteen years of study and teaching about the ancient Essenes, their insights, beliefs, and disciplines seem to me more relevant and necessary than ever. They show us a way to clear out the clutter, to cut through the frenzy of our harried lives, to find peace from the City of Peace, and to be re-created inwardly in the image of the Eternal. There is a legend that when God decided to create human beings, the angels were jealous, for they had not been privileged to share in the divine image. The angels therefore plotted to hide the divine image from human beings. One suggested burying it in the depths of the sea, another suggested hiding it in the crag of a jagged mountain peak. But the most clever of the angels suggested, "No, let us hide the divine image deep within each person. It's the last place they'll ever look!"

The scrolls themselves can be daunting and inscrutable at first approach. I have attempted here to draw from them some of the most meaningful, graspable, and spiritually suggestive passages, and to construct a series of ten disciplines from the ancient world that are relevant to contemporary life. From the masses of scroll material, I have tried to convey some of the essence of the spiritual practice of the ancient community of the Essenes—to aid us all in awakening that spark of the Eternal within.

AUTHOR'S NOTE: The citations from the Dead Sea Scrolls that appear in this book are my own translations. They are fresh, paraphrastic renderings and are markedly different from "standard" translations of the scrolls, which are most often technical and flat. I have tried to render the living sense of this material, without becoming mired in tedious and slavishly literal jargon. In the end I hope to have done justice, in contemporary style, to even the most difficult words of the Sons of Light.

1 Simplicity:
Encountering the Eternal

OCCUPY THYSELF WITH FEW THINGS,
*says the philosopher, if thou wouldst be
tranquil.... For the greatest part of what
we say and do being unnecessary, if a
man takes this away, he will have more
leisure and less uneasiness. Accordingly,
on every occasion a man should ask
himself, is this one of the unnecessary
things? Now, a man should take away
not only unnecessary acts, but also unnecessary thoughts, for thus superflu-
ous acts will not follow after.*

—Roman philosopher-emperor
Marcus Aurelius, MEDITATIONS,
Book IV, 24[1]

◇◇◇◇◇◇◇◇◇◇◇◇◇

S IMPLICITY is a goal people universally have sought across
time, but this urge has intensified as human society has
become more complex, more industrial, more technological, and much more impersonal. There must be more spiritual
abundance in life, if only we could slow our pace and teach

ourselves to get along with less materially. This theme resonates in the desert. The ancient parchments known as the Dead Sea Scrolls—perhaps more accurately labeled the "Secret Scrolls"[2]—contain a terse admonition: Embrace the wilderness; hold to your bosom the desert experiences of your life. Keep them close to you. Learn from them. It is a deep and recondite irony; for only in the experience of lack do we learn the secret of abundance.

The Secret Scrolls recount the shadowy beginnings of an ancient Judean sect who abandoned urban life to find a way in the wilderness sometime in the second century before the Common Era. They acknowledge the wilderness as a place of exile, but nonetheless a place of refuge for the weary, wayward soul. In symbolic, mystical language, we are told that a group of faithful Israelites have, by supernatural agency, been led out of one of the greatest cities in the world, Jerusalem, and into a desert of their own choosing. The Almighty thunders the following prophecy:

> *I will send the shrine of your king into exile, along with the*
> *pedestals of your statues. I will send them away from My tent....*
> —DAMASCUS RULE, col. 7:14–15

For some reason yet unknown to us, the ancient writers of the scrolls went into exile, leaving the bustling capital of ancient Judea. The Dead Sea Scrolls—the Secret Scrolls—depict something new and fresh being born from exile, as fruit of the desert, as a "fountain of living waters." When you find yourself in a desert, real or metaphorical, do not shrink from the experience. Ask what you are supposed to learn, and then seek to apply every lesson with relentless consistency. The desert is a great teacher. The only way to survive the desert is to discover the lessons it teaches—to find the "fountain of living waters." Those who fail to find it, perhaps because they fail to look, are doomed to melt in the grip of the searing heat. A Dead Sea rule book admonishes:

> *All those who have become a part of the New Covenant in*
> *the land of Damascus—but have turned aside from it, be-*
> *trayed it, and abandoned the fountain of living waters—will*
> *never be accepted in the Council of the People. They will*
> *never be inscribed in their sacred book....*
> *They are like those who have melted in the fiery furnace....*
> —DAMASCUS RULE, CD-B, col. 19:33–35; 20:3

A Land of Contrasts

Standing at the shore of the great sea of salt, you feel the blaze of the desert furnace. You are transported to a distant time; the present vanishes in the shimmering heat. Your very identity is blurred, absorbed among the members of a long-lost fraternal order. You imagine that you are one of them, heeding the call found in one of the faded, crumbling scrolls:

> *The sons of Levi, the sons of Judah, and the sons of Ben-*
> *jamin—the exiles of the desert—will go out to war against*
> *their enemies. They will battle against all their cohorts, when*
> *the exiled Sons of Light return from the Desert of the Peoples*
> *and camp in the Desert of Jerusalem....*
> —WAR RULE, col. 1:2–3

You have come to a "Jerusalem" of sorts, not the physical city of Jerusalem, a city you have abandoned, but a spiritual community—the "desert of Jerusalem." You haven't really left civilization for the desert. You have merely exchanged one desert for another. You have traded a desert of clutter and stress and oppressive tension—the "desert of the peoples"—for a desert of purity and hope.

You stand beneath the sun's blazing orb, a ridge of limestone cliffs rising to the west and the great lake of brine the ancient historian Josephus called "Asphaltis" to your immediate east. There is a starkness to the landscape that fills you with awe and reverence for the Creator of the Universe. You are in touch with your environment, in touch with yourself, in touch with God. The Dead Sea has become, in spiritual terms, a life-giving fountain:

> *I thank You, O Eternal, because You have planted my feet beside a fountain of streams. You have placed me in a parched land, beside a spring of water in a wilderness.*
> —PSALMS SCROLL, col. 16:4

You breathe in, and the very breath that you draw cleanses you. There is no impurity out here, only sand and sun and deposits of salt. All else fades away, all worldly cares vanish in the fiery heat. You are alone, yet intimately connected with a presence beyond yourself. You pause, and reflect on the nature of life. There are no distractions in this place, no obstacles to keen perception and concentration.

Suddenly the sky darkens. Heavy, moisture-laden clouds blow in from the west. Droplets turn to showers, driving rain to inundation, filling the wadis, the desert canyons, with uncontrollable torrents. But the ground cannot absorb the floods. The wadis, the barren chasms, are transformed into streaming rivers that swell and rush. As the twentieth-century Israeli poet Rakhel wrote, "And again everything flooded, and again everything stormed, breaking both the joy and the pain."[3] Just as suddenly, the storm passes, the torrents vanish, and the desert stillness returns.

It is the principle of simplicity that draws you to the wilderness. In your mind you are one more inductee into the sect called the Sons of Light, also known as the "Essenes." You are a breed apart. You are on a path different from that of the rest of humanity, even from the rest of your nation, Israel. You want life, and you want it more abundantly.

This is what you have been taught—that everyone lives in a desert of his or her own choosing. Everyone is in an exile of sorts, whether imposed or self-imposed. The only question is whether you govern the nature of your wilderness, your exile, or whether your personal desert governs you. The Secret Scrolls record your personal epiphany, the inner transformation that shapes the way you look at your desert environment:

> *The light inside my heart flows from Your wonderful myster-*
> *ies. My eyes have been privileged to gaze on eternal realities.*
> *I have beheld wisdom hidden from human beings and knowl-*
> *edge and sagacity sequestered from the sons of men. I have*
> *drunk from a fountain of righteousness and from a well of*
> *strength. I have swallowed deep drafts from a spring of glory,*
> *concealed from the assembly of flesh. . . .*
> *The track of my steps is over solid, immovable rock. The*
> *truth of the Eternal is the rock of my steps.*
> —MANUAL OF DISCIPLINE, col. 11:4–7

The simplicity you seek as you traverse the stone and sand of the desert landscape is not escape from life or its responsibilities. It is liberation, a progression to a better way. For whatever you have given up in the form of material possessions you have gained back in tranquillity, peace, order, and camaraderie.

Paradox

What was it that motivated this particular sect of ancient Judeans, bound by sacred covenant, to abandon the height of civilization and choose to live in a barren wasteland? What made them believe they could find God in the most God-forsaken place on earth? The story of the Sons of Light is in many ways a journey of paradox, of fellowship found in solitude, richness found in austerity, bounty found in simplicity. The bulk of them hailed from the greatest city in the land, a city that had come to rival Rome herself as the navel of the earth—Jerusalem. Nevertheless, residence in Jerusalem proved to be a dubious distinction; for the crushing stresses to which people were subjected in such a massive urban center were comparable to what city dwellers today face.

Without question, Jerusalem had become a gem, experiencing, by the time of King Herod the Great (reigned 37–4 B.C.E.), an explosion of growth, luxury, and opulence. There were many vast structures that adorned the great metropolis. There was an ornate Hellenistic theater, a Roman amphitheater, a vast marketplace where throngs of merchants bartered and traded, and a system of aqueducts channeling endless streams of freshwater to the burgeoning population. Three enormous towers graced the city's western approach, and a lavish palace, consisting of two huge wings encircled by a fortified enclave, had been built by King Herod. Overshadowing all was the Temple, a tremendous structure:

> *Now the temple was built of stones that were white and strong and each of their length was twenty-five cubits, their height was eight, and their breadth about twelve; and the whole structure, as also the structure of the royal cloister, was*

on each side much lower, but the middle was much higher, till
they were visible to those that dwelt in the country for a great
many furlongs....

—Josephus, ANTIQUITIES, XV, XI, 3

Who would not want to live in such a splendid place, of
which all the world sang praises? And yet there were many
who had chosen to leave Jerusalem. One gate in particular was
known as the Essene Gate, due on the one hand to the fact that
a sizable Essene population lived in Jerusalem, especially in the
vicinity of Mount Zion, and on the other hand to the fact that
so many members of the sect had left the city for good through
its limestone portals. Many inhabitants of the desert site
known as "Qumran" were originally Jerusalemites who had
become disenchanted with the busy, competitive world epito-
mized by the monstrous compound of the Temple Mount. The
ancient rule book of the sect declares:

Those people who belong to the House of Separation, and
who have departed from the Holy City ... will be judged ac-
cording to the fruit of their spirits in the Council of Holiness.

—DAMASCUS RULE, col. 20:22, 24–25

Another Dead Sea psalm refers specifically to the wilderness community—the final destination of this "House of
Separation":

You will place the foundation firmly upon rock, like mighty
beams upon the measuring-cord of justice. You stretch out the
plumb line of truth. You select tried stones, suitable for build-
ing an unshakable fortress. All who enter that fortress will
never stagger, and no enemy will ever enter it....

—PSALMS SCROLL, col. 14:25–27

The members of the community had established—with God's help—their own fortress, which rose from the sun-blanched sand. A central tower stood in the center, surrounded by a maze of plaster-covered buildings of various uses. An elaborate series of aqueducts linked the settlement with the distant hills to the west—a "fountain" of freshwater for all the inhabitants. A protective wall, which gleamed brightly in the brilliant sun, surrounded the entire compound.

Transforming the Commonplace

Among the problems city dwellers are afflicted with is the difficulty in seeing the things around them in a different light, from a higher perspective. At some point, the wonder of living disappears and with it the childlike joy of discovering new insights everywhere, in an abundance of small things. Opulence breeds complacency. The more things we have all around us, the less individual meaning any of them has. But when we withdraw to the desert, we may learn to glimpse the essential oneness in all of nature and marvel once more at the elemental powers that energize the whole of creation. We no longer take for granted the dynamic forces that seem to course through nature; and we listen carefully to the tongue with which it speaks.

In the desert we become attentive even to the winds, for they have become "angels of holiness." They whisper the mind of the Eternal:

> *You have stretched out the heavens to declare Your glory. You have established all that is in them according to Your perfect will. You made the great winds to howl, according to their laws, before they were transformed into angels of holiness, . . . the heavenly lights according to their mysteries, the stars according to their paths, and all the storm winds according to*

> *their roles—the thunder and the lightning according to their*
> *duties, and the great treasuries according to their purposes....*
> *All proceed according to their secrets.*
> —PSALMS SCROLL, col. 9:9–13

The Sons of Light practiced a daily ritual, rising well before dawn to attune their hearts and minds toward heaven in all its wonders, seeking to penetrate the mysteries, both natural and supernatural, 'round about them; for the day in which wonder is lost sight of is the day death approaches.

A study was done some years ago, in which the lives of people recognized as "geniuses," individuals of great accomplishment and impact, were evaluated in terms of their intelligence quotient, as measured by the Stanford-Binet IQ test. Surprisingly, it was discovered that the majority of them, while certainly well above average in intelligence, did not necessarily have what would be called "genius" IQs. What they did have, without exception, was the ability to look at life through the eyes of a child, always finding new mysteries to examine, new wonders to marvel at, new puzzles to solve. This is the secret of simplicity, and it is also the secret of what we call "success." The way back to joy lies in learning to transform the commonplace and make the everyday holy.

A Different Drummer

Thoreau said it well:

> *If a man does not keep pace with his companions, perhaps it*
> *is because he hears a different drummer. Let him step to the*
> *music which he hears, however measured or far away.*

The community of the Sons of Light followed a different drumbeat. The *Psalms Scroll* says:

I thank You, O Eternal, for Your eye is always fastened upon me. You have saved me from the zeal of interpreters who are full of deceit. You have rescued me from the community of those who seek smooth things.

—PSALMS SCROLL, col. 10:31–32

The Sons of Light were a society of rebels, probably viewed as outcasts by many of their contemporaries. They referred to those who reject simplicity as "those who seek smooth things." There could hardly be a better description of a society dominated by materialism. There are a good many modern "lying interpreters" who beguile us into believing that wealth and endless possessions are capable of making us truly happy. Yet study after study shows that happiness is quite disconnected from "things," and that, if anything, too many possessions make us miserable! Furthermore, numerous support groups are cropping up—voluntary simplicity societies—that aim at limiting the distractions of the age of technology-gone-mad, which tend to disorder our lives and rob us of the simple joys of living.

There is an ancient Hebrew word, *tamim,* beloved of the Sons of Light, which appears repeatedly in the Secret Scrolls, emphasizing the essential message that all of the texts teach: simplicity in all dealings. It derives from an ancient verbal root, the fundamental idea of which is completeness, wholeness, an aggregate wherein nothing is found lacking. To be *tamim* is to be "perfect," in the sense of being contented, at peace, and living in harmony with oneself and with others. It is akin to the meaning of the most famous of all Hebrew words, *shalom* ("peace"), which also describes the quality of being inwardly filled.

The Israelite prophet Ezekiel compares the inhabitants of Jerusalem to the wood of a vine, which, when it was *tamim* ("whole"), was healthy; but now it is burned, charred, and utterly useless (Ezekiel 15). The prophet is saying that the only alternative to being whole and entire, that is, inwardly complete, is being reduced to ashes. Wholeness is therefore not an option, nor is it a tangential attribute for life's journey; it is a requirement for all those who seek not merely to survive but to live abundantly.

There is, however, an additional and profoundly compelling meaning for the word *tamim*—"pure," "innocent," or "simple." How is the concept of purity related to the idea of wholeness? When the soul of the individual is full and entire, there is hardly any room for anything else—no impure motives, no corruption. Purity, therefore, is best understood as a by-product of wholeness and completion. Jesus the Nazarene would one day commend the "pure in heart, for they shall see God" (Matthew 5:8). For the Essenes, the promise was in the present tense, as they learned, day by day, the wonder of innocence, the art of ingenuousness. The *tamim* kind of simplicity does not imply a lack of sophistication; it rather suggests a lack of pretense, a lack of embellishment, a lack of affectation. A Dead Sea psalm declares:

> I thank You, O Eternal, for You have not made me dwell
> among the congregation of Vanity. You have not destined me
> to live in the council of the crafty.
> —PSALMS SCROLL, col. 15:34

To be called *tamim* in Hebrew (as might happen on the streets of Israel today) is to be labeled faultless, guileless, or even naive; it is quite the reverse of being vain or cunning. The *tamim* individual is both pure and simple, honest to a fault, sincere and unadulterated, possessing the moral fortitude to speak the truth honestly and unflinchingly.

The term appears in a number of contexts, peppered throughout the Secret Scrolls. It is usually found with another word to form terms such as "perfect of the way," "perfection of way," or "way of perfection." These same terms might just as well be translated "simple of the way," "simplicity of way," and "way of simplicity." An interesting portion of the community rule book reads:

> *As for me, my judgment is in the hands of the Eternal. In*
> *God's hand is the perfection [or simplicity] of my way.*
> *In God's hand is the righteousness of my heart.*
> —MANUAL OF DISCIPLINE, col. 11:3

This compelling psalm seems to equate simplicity with uprightness, for those whose way is "simple" (that is, "perfect") have very few roads to choose from. There is the path in the wilderness that leads to life, and there is the road of confusion, the highway of despair. The choice is simple. Elsewhere, the same psalm maintains a unique purpose coursing through nature and uniting all existence by an eternal plan, deep and profound, yet incredibly simple:

> *Without You no way is perfect [or simple]. Nothing comes to*
> *pass unless You have decreed it.*
> —MANUAL OF DISCIPLINE, col. 11:17

From Occam's Razor to Walden Pond

The importance of simplicity in all things material has been emphasized down through the centuries. One well-known exemplar was the Franciscan scholar William of Occam, who was credited with a very important postulate. It came to be known as Occam's Razor: "Entities ought not to be multiplied, except from necessity." Occam never actually made this statement. What he did say, however, is equally memorable: "It is vain to do with more what can be done with fewer." Occam systematically dissected each question as though he were brandishing a razor. In so doing, he helped to boost the concept of simplicity to the status of a formal philosophy.

The classic work on the philosophy of simplicity is Thoreau's *Walden,* hailed by many as the most important book ever written on American soil. A native of Concord, Massachusetts, Henry David Thoreau came from a middle-class, well-educated family; and while he may not have lived in the lap of luxury, he certainly hailed from the lap of civilization. He was fortunate enough to attend Harvard, which was situated only thirteen miles from his home. Returning afterward to Concord, he worked for a short time as a teacher, only to take up a career of writing, urged by his good friend and confidant, Ralph Waldo Emerson.

In due course he considered marriage, but it was not destined to be. He and his brother John were both attracted to a woman named Helen Sewell. John was the first to propose marriage to her and was also the first to be dismissed by her. Henry also proposed and was rejected as well, perhaps because Helen's father, a Unitarian minister, harbored great dislike for the radical Transcendentalist philosophy of the two brothers. Like many of the ancient Sons of Light, Thoreau remained celibate for the duration of his life. A purist in his own right, his attitude toward sex and procreation was dignified, even rarefied. In his journal, he wrote:

> *Whatever may befall me, I trust that I may never lose my respect for purity in others. The subject of sex is one on which I do not wish to meet a man at all, unless I can meet him on the most inspiring ground. I would preserve purity in act and thought as I would cherish the memory of my mother.*

Read today, this may sound prudish or inhibited, but many spiritual traditions employ periods of celibacy as part of an inward purification, an internal focusing. The Sons of Light taught similarly, as will be shown.

A defining moment in Thoreau's life took place when his brother John cut himself while shaving, developed lockjaw, and slowly died. Deeply shaken, Thoreau craved escape, a retreat to the wilderness, a journey of self-discovery. Plainspoken, yet highly passionate and emotive—traits he inherited from his mother—Thoreau would not be content with the genteel observations offered up in the voluminous literary notebook he had been compiling. He decided to put the busy and competitive life of polite society behind him. He had to live the things he wrote:

> *I want to go soon and live away by the pond, where I shall hear only the wind whispering among the reeds. I will be a success if I have left myself behind. But my friends ask what I will do when I get there. Will it not be employment enough to watch the progress of the seasons?*

Therefore, on the Fourth of July in the year 1845, Henry David Thoreau made a personal declaration of independence, retreating to a tract of land owned by Emerson, situated near a quiet pond called Walden. There he built a small cabin, where he would compose the greatest work of his life:

> *I lived alone in the woods a mile from any people, in a house which I built myself, on the shore of Walden Pond, in Concord, Massachusetts, and earned my living by the labor of my hands.*

For the next two years, two months, and two days, he kept a journal that would form the core of his masterpiece, *Walden*.

It was, as he described it, a personal attempt to simplify his life, to limit his expenditures, and to observe the wonder of nature with due care and scrutiny. More than this, it was a spiritual journey, a metaphysical quest to find true personhood. It was a stepping out of the "rat race," to find meaning, value, and above all, simplicity. He observed:

> Our life is frittered away by detail. An honest man has hardly
> need to count more than his ten fingers; or in extreme cases,
> he may add his ten toes, and lump the rest.

The book's seventeen chapters are the quintessence of pithy conciseness. A clear response to the excesses of the Industrial Revolution, Thoreau's private journey is the spiritual descendant of the grand experiment launched two millennia before by a group who called themselves only the Sons of Light and who had responded to the slavery and excess of their own day. "God's drop" is how Thoreau described Walden Pond. What Thoreau wrote about his favorite pond could well have been written by the ancient Essenes about the Dead Sea:

> It is glorious to behold this ribbon of water sparkling
> in the sun.

Walden meant something sacred to him, just as the desert was sacred to the Sons of Light. Like them, he searched for true spirituality. Like them, he sought to find the resonance of the Eternal in untamed stretches of wilderness. As with the Sons of Light, his experience of wilderness life would lead to a literary legacy destined to inspire the world forever.

In 1847 Thoreau returned to Concord, devoting several additional years to writing and rewriting *Walden*. In 1862 he developed tuberculosis and, as he lay dying, was asked if he had made his peace with God. His classic response is remembered to this day: "We never quarreled."

Of their relationship to God, the Sons of Light wrote, with depth and conviction:

> *I have loved You freely, with all my heart. I have meditated deeply on the mysteries of Your wisdom.... I have loved You freely, with all my heart and with all my soul.*
>
> —PSALMS SCROLL, col. 6:26–27; 7:13

The Tonic of Wildness

The Essenes did not live an entirely primitive existence in their desert stronghold. We know this not only from what ancient historians have written about the sect but also from the archaeology of the desert site called Qumran. For when the rubble was removed in the 1950s and the Essene "headquarters" was uncovered in its entirety, a surprising level of sophistication was also revealed.

As a covenantal society, they were not impoverished hermits, living in complete austerity. Their settlement was in fact a marvel of architectural prowess, on a par with anything the classical world had been able to produce. There were stately Hellenistic columns, fine pottery, and imported glassware. And the elaborate aqueduct system was an amazing feat of engineering. The compound the Sons of Light built was in fact so impressive that a team of modern archaeologists, returning to the site, declared that a place as sophisticated as this could not have been the domicile of the Essenes. A new theory, advanced in recent years, is that Qumran must instead have been the site of a wealthy Roman villa!

But those who question whether the Sons of Light ever resided here tend to forget that living in the wilderness, in

touch with nature and with the Eternal, does not mean aban-
doning civilized life. It merely means striking a balance between civilization on the one hand and nature on the other.
Thoreau is a case in point, for while he lived at Walden Pond
for two years, he regularly took walks into town, built a fine
(though simple) cabin for himself, and chose to live comfort-
ably, even in the woods. Like the Essenes, Thoreau was loathe
to become a hermit. Walden Pond was just over a mile from
Concord itself, and he made sure that he had society at his
elbow. But he understood the necessity of retreat, the need to
live in tune with the natural world. "My profession," he wrote,
"is to be always on the alert to find God in nature, to know His
lurking places, to attend all the oratorios, the operas, in nature." In other words, we need the "tonic of wildness."
Moreover, experiencing wildness *enhances* our civilized life; it
does not replace it.

It appears that Qumran was not the only place Essene societies thrived; there were pockets of Essenes scattered everywhere. It appears that in Jerusalem, the vicinity of Mount Zion
was a major Essene "quarter," where members of the sect clus-
tered together in a society of their own. While they surely
looked to Qumran for guidance, they chose to stay where they
were, applying desert simplicity to urban Jerusalem. But even
those who remained in the cities of Judea made periodic pil-
grimages to the wilderness, to participate in the great annual
festival of the Renewal of the Covenant. They camped in tents
near Lake Asphaltis and drank of the tonic of wildness. It was
an ancient version of a spiritual retreat. Something in human
nature requires the tonic of wildness to restore the soul.

Re-forming the Individual

> *As for me, who am I? I am but a creature made of clay,*
> *kneaded with water ... with an ear of dust and a heart of*
> *stone. What am I to be worthy of this?*
> —PSALMS SCROLL, col. 21:10–11

The Essenes had gone to the desert, not to live simply for simplicity's sake alone, but, in that simplicity, to encounter the Eternal. Encounter was at the heart of their collective life, and they were wise enough to recognize the price that must be paid for it. The Sons of Light understood that encounter implies change; it necessitates reformation and expands the possibility of the single self. They understood that you cannot reform whole communities, nor can you reform crowds. You reform individuals, and you do it one at a time. You reform yourself. It is reformed individuals who build reformed communities.

A result of encounter with the Divine Presence is a heightened experience of self. It amounts to "being lived" as much as merely living. In finding the Eternal, I find a "philosophic Other," who puts me in tune with myself. In other words, I am free to be fully me, because I am intimately connected with One who is wholly other. As the twentieth-century philosopher Martin Buber wrote, "I require a You to become me. . . . All actual life is encounter."[4] Therefore when we fail to experience transcendental moments of encounter, we miss out on "actual life." We may be alive, but we are not truly living.

What we need to do, then, is not merely seek "reform" in the abstract; we need actively to *re-form* ourselves on a regular basis. *Re-formation* is at the heart of the growth process, and it comes only by determined effort. Pop philosophy is of little use in embarking on a personal journey to the wilderness. More-over, the journey will most assuredly be a disconcerting one, the divine encounter putting us in touch with our own essential weakness, for we are all but "creatures of clay."

Paradoxically it is in the simplicity of our weakness that we discover our simple greatness. As we re-form ourselves, one by one, we also re-form our families, our communities, the planet. The voice of the re-formed individual becomes charged with the spirit of zeal:

> *I will always be a spirit of zeal, standing resolute in the face*
> *of the seekers of smooth things. All the men of deceit may*
> *murmur against me. They sound like the roaring of many*
> *waters....*
>
> *But You have established me firmly, like a banner for the*
> *Elect of justice. You have made me a sage interpreter of many*
> *wondrous mysteries....*
>
> —PSALMS SCROLL, col. 10:13, 15–16

2 Community:
Tapestry of the Living

RATIONAL ANIMALS EXIST FOR ONE
another....
That which is not good for the swarm,
neither is it good for the bee.

—Marcus Aurelius, MEDITATIONS,
Book IV, 3; Book VI, 54

◇◇◇◇◇◇◇◇◇◇◇◇

T HE SHELTERED, ordered community of Qumran may seem distant and ideal in the light of contemporary life, but the human condition, and basic issues of identity and the human spirit, are unchanging.

A low rumble of angst is propelling us into the new millennium. People feel more alienated than ever, like children lost in the midst of a great crowd. Significantly, the leading cause of death of young adults, right behind car crashes, isn't guns or drugs; it is suicide. Amazingly, suicide among the young appears to be a uniquely Western, industrialized phenomenon. Compare the rate of self-murder in the industrial West with suicide rates in the less industrial "developing world," and we find that they are not to be compared at all. Even in lands where the population suffers deprivation, malnutrition, and even starvation, suicide is very scarce. Why, then, do so many who live in relative luxury despair? Perhaps it all boils down to a precipitous loss of identity and the breakdown of social and familial structures.

Social structures are an integral part of the animal kingdom; our closest primate relatives, the chimpanzees, are a superb case in point. The herding instinct is so much a part of animal behavior, especially of "higher primates," that chimpanzees, who in the wild live in actual families within "tribal" groups, when taken into captivity enter a kind of living death. They shun reproduction and sometimes starve themselves, literally giving up and dying.[5] Similar behavior has also been observed among other large mammals, from big cats to elephants to giraffes. Clearly group separation, as one aspect of living in captivity, has deadly consequences.

So it is with human beings when societal bonds, known in so-called primitive cultures as "tribes," weaken and disintegrate. Strong tribal affiliation gives each individual member the sense that he or she matters, that the well-being of the individual is essential to the well-being of the community—the "tribe," the "Many." The need to belong is one of the most powerful drives we have. Whether living amid urban sprawl or the plethora of "little boxes" most typical of suburban housing, very few people have more than the slightest connection with their neighbors, aside from a polite wave of the hand on driving off to work. It is a sad phenomenon.

The Sons of Light felt that without community, without "the Many,"[6] we die. They believed that the society they had known in Jerusalem had grown corrupt, despotic, and defiled by impurity. Their answer was to build a desert community where they could start from scratch. The pure community they helped establish in the wilderness would in turn inspire those who chose to remain in the cities. Their lot was to teach by example. They were, by anyone's estimation, a "tribe." They labored together, prayed together, copied their holy books together, participated in ritual bathings together, took their meals together.

Utopia on the Bitter Lake

The community to which the Sons of Light joined themselves was a utopia of sorts, though located in some of the most inhospitable territory on the surface of the planet. Hardly a lush, tropical paradise or a high mountain refuge, the desert settlement they called home was a place where the air hung thick with a sulfurous effluvium that seemed to rise from the earth itself and where the unblinking eye of heaven withered every living thing.

They lived modestly, unpretentiously. They who called themselves Sons of Light are aptly described, inasmuch as the brilliant heaven above bleached the desert floor with such a blinding radiance as to lay bare the very soul of everyone who dared to inhabit this unforgiving turf. To be a Son of Light was to welcome the glistening rays, allowing their illumination to flood every dark corner of their inner being. But beyond this, those who joined themselves to "the Many" needed to apprehend, like the rising and setting of the sun itself, the patterns and rhythms of daily life in the great rift valley. They needed to appreciate the unique habitat they had chosen, along with the organizational patterns that their environment naturally engendered.

Agriculture

It all began with the earth and the produce thereof. Farming, like all other aspects of communal life, was a collective endeavor. There were no private plots; everything proceeded for the good of the whole community. A few kilometers to the south of the settlement (at a place known today as Ein Feshka), the arid landscape was brought to life through the remarkable effects of irrigation. All able-bodied individuals joined in the common cause: to pick out the stones, to till the soil, to channel the precious life-giving streams through a network of canals. The young plants were tended by a joint watchfulness, each seedling brought to maturity through common labor. Harvests were communal projects, and in the end the fruit of the fields belonged to the whole.

Tilling the soil united the entire community with the natural environment, across the ongoing cycle of the seasons. To bring forth life in a land of death was to witness a series of daily miracles as each kernel sprouted, as each shoot pushed upward, as each green leaf appeared, and as each flower opened toward the daylight. For the Sons of Light there was a powerful messianic overtone to the tilling of the ground and the fresh sprouts that such labor brought forth:

> You have established a Plantation—of cypress trees, pines, with cedars, planted together, to Your glory. They are trees of life by a secret fountain, sequestered among all the trees at waterside. They will cause a Shoot to blossom in the eternal Plantation. They will take root before they blossom. They stretch their roots out to the water channel; their trunks extend to living waters. They will become an eternal spring....

> The One who makes the Branch of holiness to flower—in the Plantation of truth—hides it, un-esteemed and unknown. Its secret is sealed.... But You, O Eternal, have preserved its fruit, along with the secret of the heroes of might and the spirits of holiness. The swirling, fiery flames will never touch the fountain of life, or harm the eternal trees.

> —PSALMS SCROLL, col. 16:5–8, 10–12

Settlements

"Beautiful for situation, the joy of the whole earth" is the biblical description of Mount Zion (Psalm 48:2). The same words might equally apply to the Zion of the wilderness. The settlement the Sons of Light built consisted of a central compound of buildings adorning the western shore of the great bitter lake.[7] From what we know today about the archaeological remains of the site, we can imagine what the settlement was like two millennia ago.

A protective wall completely surrounded the compound, assembled, along with all the other structures, from smoothly cut limestone blocks, covered in plaster. The wall was ample to protect the settlement from wild beasts and marauders, but not particularly suited to fending off armed forces. A fortified tower, of square proportions better suited to defense, marked the center of the northern wall.

From the northwest an aqueduct fed water into the compound, filling a series of large cisterns and ritual immersion baths as the channel wended its course between the structures. It was a marvel of ancient engineering, suggesting that the settlement was no paupers' refuge but the hub of a prosperous, technologically advanced society. The aqueduct and cisterns seemed strangely out of place in the midst of this harsh and barren landscape. They formed striking patterns of blue in stark contrast with the prevailing chalky turf.

Among the buildings along which the canal passed stood a long, rectangular assembly hall and refectory, where communal meals were served for scores of Essenes, joined in holy purpose. On the other side of the artificial stream, there was a kitchen and pantry, with hundreds of neatly stacked dishes. A potter's kiln was found nearby; it was used for firing the many vessels required for cooking and storage. There were stables for

horses; there was a laundry, where garments were trod under-
foot and cleansed in the sparkling water. Most importantly,
there was another rectangular chamber, a "scriptorium,"
where a great library of the accumulated wisdom and knowledge of centuries was meticulously hand-copied by those who
served as scribes, laboring all day, every day, seated at a series
of plaster-covered benches.

The inhabitants made use of the buildings, not for sleeping,
but for worship, for writing, studying, and copying their holy
books, and for communal meals, served during the daylight
hours. Hellenistic columns adorned some of the structures, emphasizing the stylish prosperity of this curiously secluded outpost. By night they reposed not in the stately stone buildings but
in caves dotting the nearby cliffs as well as in tents surrounding
the sacred precincts. Only after a lengthy period of probation
(two or three years) were initiates allowed to enter the hallowed East Gate, which greeted the blazing sun at its rising and
equally stood sentinel for the soon-coming Messiah, who, they
believed, would make his approach from the same direction.

The central compound of the settlement was certainly the
"headquarters" and focal point of this desert sect, but in the
Essene Quarter of Jerusalem, and in the other groupings of
Essenes across Judea, the community atmosphere was pro-
nounced—the sense of extended families, living, as it were, a
single, shared life and taking meals together, from house to
house. Equally conspicuous were the communal storehouses,
where grains and other food items were deposited for the
shared use of all, as well as for traveling emissaries, who linked
the settlements in a great network of mutual communication.

Officials and Magistrates

There was no sense of tyranny in this sequestered society. The congregation as a whole elected its leaders, who served as judges for a specific period of time. Four of them were of priestly descent (born from the consecrated tribe of Levi); the other six were laypeople. Charisma was no qualification among the Sons of Light. The major prerequisite for service involved being deeply schooled in a mysterious, lost volume called the *Book of Meditation*.[8] Unless it is someday found among the silent caves of the great Jordan River rift valley (at the bottom of which sits the Dead Sea), we will never know its contents. But it is clear that wisdom and knowledge were highly prized among the Sons of Light.

These judges were to be between twenty-five and sixty years old. Each was to be given leadership responsibility in proportion to his maturity. The same held true for all other positions of responsibility. In the hierarchical society of the Sons of Light, specific age requirements were set forth as follows:

> At the age of twenty-five years, he will take his place among the administrators of the Community of Holiness, to undertake the work of the community. At the age of thirty years, he will be mature enough to adjudicate disputes and judgments. He will take his place among the leaders of the thousands of Israel—the princes of the hundreds, the princes of the fifties, the princes of the tens—who act as judges and magistrates for their tribes, in all their families, by warrant of the sons of Aaron, the priests. Every chief among the clans of the community (to whom the lot has fallen) will share the obligation of going out and coming in before the community, according to his wisdom and the perfection of his way. He will dedicate himself to be faithful in accomplishing his tasks among his fellows. A person will honor one

comrade more than another, according to whether this dedica-
tion is much or little.
—MESSIANIC RULE, col. 1:12–18

Bear in mind that this utopia—while laying claim to being an ideal society—didn't shirk responsibility; it embraced it, challenging every individual to welcome the obligations of age, to accept the yoke that maturity brings. Administratively the tasks were to be broken down, the units of governance taking responsibility for increasingly intimate assemblages, from groups of a thousand, to one hundred, to just ten.

Riding herd over all was an individual known as the "Overseer," one who had taken up the spiritual mantle of the distant founder of the community, known as the "Teacher of Righteousness." It was the Overseer who instructed the desert flock "to live according to the Book of the Community Rule," and who evaluated the metaphysical progress of the new initi- ates into the holy order of the Sons of Light. The idea of a wise elder presiding over an ideal society is frequently found in utopian literature, all the way back to Plato. Such a leader was not a despot, nor was this leader a hereditary monarch. The Overseer exercised moral authority, translating the rule of law into a compassionate dominion of justice for all:

THIS IS THE MANUAL FOR THE OVERSEER OF THE COMMUNITY:
He will teach the Many of the works of the Eternal and will
give them understanding of the Eternal's mighty acts.... He
will show them mercy, as a father is compassionate toward
his children. He will give water to them in all their affliction,
like a shepherd who faithfully tends his flock. He will release
the chains that hold them captive, so that no one will be trou-
bled or dejected in all the community.
—DAMASCUS RULE, col. 13:7–10

Community Life

While the family remained the basic component of society among the Essenes outside Qumran, for the elite spiritual community on the shore of the Dead Sea, celibacy was the rule, and wives were not allowed. It appears that the Sons of Light so deadened their physical passions, so dedicated their hearts to pursuing disciplined lives, that they lived as celibates as long as they remained at Lake Asphaltis. This is what the historian Josephus reports, yet some of the graves excavated at Qumran have been found to contain the skeletal remains of women. Researchers are divided on the whole question of whether women lived at Qumran. I suggest that the Essenes argued about this point, reaching a compromise decision that in the cities and towns of Judea, where they lived in widely scattered groups, they would rear children and raise families. Something about the celibate lifestyle has made it particularly suited to religious, isolated communities down through history, from medieval monasteries to such diverse groups as the Shakers, the Rappites, and others. In the case of the Dead Sea headquarters, disciples had to be recruited from young men prepared to consecrate themselves to this life. The Secret Scrolls contain this phrase, which seems to speak of the adoption of young people into the sect:

> *You have established me as a father to the Sons of Loving-kindness. I have become like a nursemaid to the men of miracles. They open their mouths like a baby at its mother's breast—like a playful child in its nursemaid's lap.*
> —PSALMS SCROLL, col. 15:20–22

If we believe that the Essenes at Qumran were celibate males, then we would assume that these adoptees were boys only. Abstinence was highly prized, and youth were taught to restrain their passions for the good of themselves and the community at large.

There was a marked egalitarian quality to the lonely, arid paradise where the Sons of Light resided, for every individual was a coworker with his fellow. There was of course a certain hierarchy of elders, and younger members of the community paid due deference to those who were more mature. The old, far from being pushed to the periphery of society, were crowned with honor and deepest respect:

> *When a man begins to get old, he will be assigned duties in*
> *the community according to his level of strength.*
> —MESSIANIC RULE, col. 1:19

Every society in the human family has some designated age of maturity, at which time a person legally passes from childhood to adulthood. As Jewish society has evolved, that age is thirteen, at which time a young Jewish male or female can say, "Now I am a man," or "Now I am a woman." Among the Sons of Light, accustomed to longevity and equally accustomed to cultivating the attribute of patience, that age was twenty:

> *When he is twenty years old, he will pass the threshold of*
> *maturity, taking on his appointed tasks among his family and*
> *officially joining the Community of Holiness. . . . Afterwards,*
> *he will be allowed to give testimony regarding the judgments*
> *of the Law. He will be called upon in the announcement of*
> *statutes.*
> —MESSIANIC RULE, col. 1:8–9, 11

When life expectancy was short, there seemed to be a compelling need to hurry along rites of passage, to bring individuals into society as full-fledged "adults" as quickly as possible.

But for the Essenes out in the desert there was plenty of time. While the modern world is terribly impatient, the Sons of Light learned so to moderate their living that time itself seemed to slow down for them. Perhaps they simply realized that the key to appreciating anything is cultivating the ability to wait for it.

A precise rhythm of daily life provided each member of the community with an inward equanimity—an anchor of the soul that coalesced with the routine of every twenty-four-hour period. At the so-called fifth hour of each day (which came at noon), those who labored returned to the central compound to take their repast together. The daily meal was a holy gathering, a priestly convocation, which required that all should bathe themselves in ritual immersion baths prior to eating. Their work clothes were exchanged for a loincloth, whereupon they descended a series of plaster-covered steps into an elaborate water-filled cistern. Now cleansed, they climbed up again, like newborn babes, refreshed and regenerated for the banquet to follow.

The great feast was more than a meal. It was a repast of profound significance, for it cemented the whole community in a high and holy vision of spiritual equality, preserved under divine protection. Symbolically, in their joint consumption of the staff of life, those who dined together declared their solidarity. It was a daily way of proclaiming the idea of "covenant," a contract between the people and God. The people agreed to carry out their just responsibilities, and the Eternal in return agreed to offer protection "under the shadow" of the divine presence. The people's faith and the divine protection, twin pillars of the desert covenant, kept them and sustained them.

The Essenes' rigid rules of purity might seem a harsh form of religious legalism. But looked upon another way, they simply embody the highest values of personal cleanliness and hygiene, making sure that one's body is cleansed in water on a daily basis. The Sons of Light comprised an ancient order of "purists," who practiced the admonition "Cleanliness is next to godliness" long before it was generally convenient to do so.

Economy

The wilderness community experienced by the Sons of Light involved a sharing of life in general and equally a sharing of resources. As with other utopian formulations across the historical record, no one was to call anything his or her own, but all material wealth was held in common. They understood that just as power corrupts, so does money. The drive for dominance becomes wedded to the drive for possessions and for capital. Therefore, they were admonished, place capital in the hands of the whole, not in the hands of individuals, and the whole face of the community will be redefined.

The ancient world in which the Essenes lived was certainly not without its slaves, many of whom labored to build King Herod the Great's architectural marvels. Those who were not physically enslaved often felt spiritually and psychically enslaved by a corrupt religious establishment presiding in Jerusalem's temple and by a diabolical police state that scrutinized their every word and every movement.

"Separate yourselves from the peoples of the land!" said the high priest Ezra, and this is precisely what the Sons of Light did. The many rules and proscriptions for communal living laid down in the scrolls indicate that the goods of the community were held and shared communally. Just as their labors were shared, so were the fruits of their labors, the produce of their fields, and all financial and economic gain. All property and possessions held prior to joining the community were funneled into the common treasury. The members of the community contributed to the common cause according to their ability and received from the common treasury according to their needs. No one felt the need to amass great personal wealth; for a person's life consists not in the abundance of the things he or she possesses.

The Tapestry of the Living

One complete Dead Sea scroll, the *Psalms Scroll,* is a remarkable collection of Hebrew poetry of biblical style, unknown to the world until discovered by the Bedouin in 1947. It addresses many themes, from the praise of the exalted God to the inadequacy of human beings. Particularly revealing is the attitude toward those who live outside the bounds of the ancient society, whose lives, caught up in the torment of the world beyond, seem hopeless in comparison to the simple joys found among the redeemed community:

> *All of their wise men are like sailors, tossed to and fro on the wild seas. All their "wisdom" has been swallowed by the resounding roar of the ocean. The deeps bubble and boil above the great fountains, unleashing enormous waves and huge breakers, which fume with deafening timbre. When they roll forward, Hell and Destruction open their mouths.*
> —PSALMS SCROLL, col. 11:14–16

The world built by the Essenes was fundamentally different. Indeed, the most striking thing about those who called themselves Sons of Light was not their military muscle or even their proud settlement—the remains of which still adorn the desert valley, twenty centuries later—but their fraternity, their deep level of mutual commitment. The ancient historian wrote:

> *They have no certain city, but many of them dwell in every city;*
> *and if any of their sect come from other places, what they have*
> *lies open for them, just as if it were their own; and they go into*
> *such as they never knew before, as if they had been ever so long*
> *acquainted with them.*
> —Josephus, WARS, II, VIII, 4

He also wrote:

> *There are about four thousand men that live in this way, and*
> *neither marry wives, nor are desirous to keep servants; as think-*
> *ing the latter tempts men to be unjust, and the former gives the*
> *handle to domestic quarrels; but as they live by themselves, they*
> *minister one to another.*
> —Josephus, ANTIQUITIES, XVIII, I, 5

They came to this stark moonscape of sand and rock, and a great stone encampment, snugly situated along the northwest shore of Lake Asphaltis—the Dead Sea. Their settlement graced the dusty shore between the bitter lake and the chalky marl cliffs in the distance, where the sun slides into oblivion at the end of each searing desert day. The land itself has been swallowed up in the mighty Jordan River rift valley, a geological fault line that has sunk the entire lake and all its environs to more than twelve hundred feet below sea level. From the Judean hills in the west to the mountains of Moab in the east, this enormous crevasse holds the visitor in its dusty grip. There is an eternal stillness here, and a solitude that penetrates the bones. However, the Sons of Light did not set out to leave humanity but to join themselves to a company of others of like mind, fully prepared to cement, by holy covenant, life into life.

An ancient hymn in the *Psalms Scroll* expresses their deepest thanksgiving:

> *I thank You, O Eternal, for having knotted up my soul in the*
> *tapestry of the living!*
> —PSALMS SCROLL, col. 10:20

People today often live their lives in the midst of urban congestion and yet feel isolated, lonely, and alienated, even from those closest to them. We long to be that single necessary thread in an intricate and ornate fabric, whose full beauty becomes apparent only from a distance—the "tapestry of the living."

One Harvard psychiatrist writes pointedly about the need for a "feeling that you belong, that you're a part of something larger than yourself."[9] Be it a family, a neighborhood, a classroom, or a deep friendship, it is vital for emotional health that we feel that we belong, that we are wanted, that we are "connected." Furthermore, the deeper the relationship, the more positive the health consequences will be. Increasing numbers of studies have provided hard data, indicating that the more connected a person is, the more likely that individual will be to live a long and healthy life. Physiology is affected. The autoimmune system is affected. There is no more important goal in the technological age than for us to strive for the human moment—interpersonal, face-to-face connectedness.

When the Sons of Light left Jerusalem, they were not merely rejecting the city they had known and loved. They were seeking to build a different sort of city, whose physical dimensions were only a reflection of a much grander community. Together they called themselves "the Many." The settlement known today as Qumran may have been the locus of the community—its physical headquarters—but it was not the community itself. The true community ("the Many") was invisible, incorporeal. It consisted of souls knit together, not just bodies. At its nucleus were the spirits of all of those who had come to the wilderness. But like concentric waves from a pebble striking Lake Asphaltis, the network they called Essene extended to kindred souls scattered across the land, from Jerusalem to Judea to Samaria, and places far beyond.

Community isn't a theory; it is a practice, a discipline, which means that it is a skill to be learned. If something is to be learned, there must be a teacher, and there once was a great righteous teacher. All the Sons of Light were taught a great deal about this "Teacher of Righteousness," though he died—cut down by an act of treachery—not long after the community was founded. But some of his immediate disciples survived him, deriving their authority from having known him, having imbibed his teachings about the Many, about community and fraternity and love. The Teacher's immediate presence was expressed by one they called the Overseer. It was he who expressed the dynamic of the Teacher's soul, which still energized the disciples. It was he who interpreted and applied the many laws that govern human interaction, from the precise observance of the Sabbath, to the treatment of animals, to harboring grudges against one's fellow. Community is a difficult discipline, but it strengthens us, guides us, and makes us whole.

This is why many in ancient Judea chose the way of the Sons of Light. For all they may have had to sacrifice—the creature comforts of the great and holy city—the sense of belonging that pervaded the community made up for everything. They became meaningful members of the greater assembly. Each took his identity from the whole, of which he was a meaningful part. By contrast, the world outside seemed chaotic, unsettled, and dangerous.

Fellowship — "Fellows in the Same Ship"

When it comes to this uniquely bonded community, the *Psalms Scroll* employs images of a ship traversing stormy seas and of a mighty fortress, secure before the enemy:

> *My soul is like a ship, amidst the howling seas. I am like a*
> *fortress-city, in the face of furious enemies.*
> —PSALMS SCROLL, col. 11:6–7

Elsewhere, there is the stunning image of the Eternal—the King—being equivalent with the community itself:

> *The King is the congregation!*
> —DAMASCUS RULE, frag. 3, col. 3:18

So dominant is the theme of community that a number of different Hebrew words are used in the scrolls to delineate its important functions: the *Kahal* (קהל), the *Edah* (עדה), the *Yakhad* (יחד), and the *Rabim* (רבים). The first term, *Kahal* (קהל), is normally translated "assembly," though it most likely derives from an ancient root word, *Kol* (קול), which means "to speak" or "voice." The idea is that people are assembled vocally, to receive instruction, which is spoken, verbally, into their ears. They are to be taught, trained in the path to follow. The second term, *Edah* (עדה), refers to gathering together for the purpose of testifying to revealed truth and proclaiming a great witness. An *Edah* is a witnessing body that sets an example for the rest of the world. The third term, *Yakhad* (יחד), implies unity, oneness, an indivisible, incorruptible joining of heart and soul and purpose. Even the Eternal is called by a derivative of this word, *Ekhad* (אחד) or "One."[10] In this most mystical sense, God, who is called "the King," *is* the congregation, and the congregation *is* the King. Perhaps most important is the term *Rabim*

(רבים), the Many, suggesting multiplicity and diversity. It is the embodiment of the motto of the United States: *E pluribus unum*—From many, one. These four themes epitomize for the Essenes what community was all about: verbal instruction, setting an example, and becoming one from many.

As another ancient sage of the Mediterranean world would write:

> *All things are implicated with one another, and the bond is holy; and there is hardly anything unconnected with any other thing.*
> —Marcus Aurelius, MEDITATIONS, Book VII, 9

The ancient historian also tells us of the rigor of communal life among the Sons of Light in tones so unflinching as to disconcert our modern sensibilities:

> *Now after the time of their preparatory trial is over, they are parted into four classes; and so far are the juniors inferior to the seniors, that if the seniors should be touched by the juniors, they must wash themselves, as if they had intermixed themselves with the company of a foreigner.*
> —Josephus, WARS, II, VIII, 10

Doubtless, wherever there is "tribe," there will be hierarchy, levels of commitment, and privileges based on those levels. But the Many were kept in line by unflinching discipline and an admirable devotion to "virtue." There was a recognition that without the community, people die:

> *But for those that are caught in any heinous sins, they cast them out of their society; and he who is thus separated from them, does often die after a miserable manner; for as he is bound by*

*the oath he hath taken, and by the customs he hath been engaged
in, he is not at liberty to partake of that food that he meets with
elsewhere, but is forced to eat grass, and to famish his body with
hunger till he perish; for which reason they receive many of them
again when they are at their last gasp, out of compassion to
them, as thinking the miseries they have endured till they come
to the very brink of death to be a sufficient punishment for the
sins they had been guilty of.*

—Josephus, WARS, II, VIII, 8

Single and Serene

All the benefits of community notwithstanding, one of the
most puzzling, yet profound aspects of this exclusive order is
described by the historian in the following terms:

*They neglect wedlock, but choose out other persons' children,
while they are pliable, and fit for learning; and esteem them to be
of their kindred, and form them according to their own manners.
They do not absolutely deny the fitness of marriage, and the suc-
cession of mankind thereby continued; but they guard against . . .
lascivious behavior. . . .*

—Josephus, WARS, II, VIII, 2

The call to celibacy among the Sons of Light (at least at the
main settlement on the shore of Lake Asphaltis) is probably the
most alien aspect of Essene life to contemporary minds. Resis-
tance to the idea of celibacy is one reason the Catholic priesthood is in precipitous decline. We ought to pause, however, and
consider what those who chose celibacy desired to teach
through this most difficult lifestyle. One of the most problem-
atic maladies besetting modern people in a climate of alienation
is the idea that true happiness is to be found in someone else's

arms. Whether it is women desperately seeking eligible bachelors or men constantly on the lookout for the right kind of women, a definitively modern mania is the idea that romantic couplehood is some kind of panacea. Increasingly, singles are being admonished as follows: Reevaluate your station in life and learn to love yourself rather than getting trapped in a desperate "search mode" for Mr. or Ms. right. You don't have to take a vow of celibacy, but neither should you look to the perfect relationship as the answer to life's challenges.

Many males in our culture have a particularly hard time establishing meaningful friendships. Women have an average of six close friends with whom they can share intimate details of life. Men, aside from their partners, have none. The insular, "friendless" male is the rule rather than the exception in modern society. Male friendships tend to be shallow and superficial, barely getting past the sports news. Little wonder that a men's movement has surfaced in the last decade, organized by men seeking to crack the macho veneer and to bond with one another.

Perhaps moderns can look to the Sons of Light as an ancient version of a "male bonding society," seeking to penetrate the coldness of a very inhuman age.

"Like a Dream behind Me"

The society the Sons of Light created was more than a religious order. It was utopian in many ways, fabricated ex nihilo, seemingly from the dust itself. Utopian societies, by their very definition, do not exist. Yet visions of ideal communities have stirred our collective psyche from the very beginning of civilization. Concrete attempts have been made to found and nurture various alternative communities from antiquity to the present day. In America in particular, utopian visions and experiments have abounded from the beginning. Ralph Waldo Emerson wrote in the mid-1800s that there was "not a reading man but has a draft of a new community in his pocket."

The most famous American utopia of all was called Brook Farm, an outgrowth of the Transcendentalist movement of Ralph Waldo Emerson, John Greenleaf Whittier, and other New England notables. Envisioned by a Unitarian minister named George Ripley and celebrated in a novel by Nathaniel Hawthorne, Brook Farm was to mingle the ideas of simplicity of lifestyle and profundity of thought. Its community school received students from far and wide. The community was officially commissioned in the year 1844, but its vitality was sapped when a catastrophic fire destroyed its central building just two years later. Like so many other bold experiments, Brook Farm slowly expired. Hawthorne well caught the essence of American utopias and their slow dissolution when he wrote of Brook Farm, "It already looks like a dream behind me."[11]

Given the challenges of utopian communities, it is all the more astounding that a desert community, living on one of the most inhospitable landscapes on the planet over two millennia ago, would not only survive but prosper, thrive, and flourish, not for a decade or two, but for two long centuries.

3 Vision:
Ordering the Mind

THE ESSENCE OF LEADERSHIP IS A
vision you articulate clearly and force-
fully on every occasion. You can't blow
an uncertain trumpet.

—Theodore Hesburgh

◇◇◇◇◇◇◇◇◇◇◇◇◇

PERSPECTIVE, say the wise, is the most challenging thing in life to achieve, the most difficult to maintain, and the easiest to lose. Certainly there are many circumstances in our lives that we did not create and over which we have no control. But we have it entirely within our power to determine how we look at our own existence and how we evaluate the meaning, purpose, and significance of our lives, in whatever condition we find ourselves. When clutter presses in, when responsibilities mount, when the frenetic pace of living crowds the freedom of our thought, we may find ourselves distracted, unable to come to grips with the things that are really important in life. Putting our minds in good order is the most important discipline we can acquire. As the Roman sage and emperor Marcus Aurelius wrote:

I affirm that tranquillity is nothing else than the good ordering
of the mind. . . . Let thy principles be brief and fundamental,
which as soon as thou shalt recur to them, will be sufficient to
cleanse the soul completely, and to send thee back free from all
discontent with the things to which thou returnest.
—Marcus Aurelius, MEDITATIONS, Book IV, 3

The Secret Scrolls from the Judean desert put it another
way:

Give heed, you wise ones—you who meditate on knowledge.
You who are hurried and overwrought, be of steady purpose.
Add cleverness to your minds. You who are just and righteous,
be done with vice and turpitude. And all you Perfect of the Way,
lift up the poor and downtrodden. Learn patience and long-
suffering, and accept all righteous judgments!
—PSALMS SCROLL, col. 9:34–37

Those who joined themselves to the covenant became
members of "the Many." They were far removed from Jerusalem in spirit if not in sheer distance. Their brave little settlement, opposite Lake Asphaltis, was a universe apart, full of
wonder and magic and vivid dreams. The desert "moonscape"
had become a "dreamscape." The corporeal world—of struggle, of rage and rancor, of domination, of political turmoil—
tapered into oblivion, replaced by the vast stillness of the rift
valley. The crisp, cool air of the mornings cleansed the spirit, as
each individual would rise well before dawn to breathe in the
fullness of each new day. Others must have seen the empty valley and the bitter lake as an open wound in the earth's crust,
but not the bold compatriots of Qumran. To them the earth
seemed young and fresh, virtually "newborn" in this great

crevasse, unspoiled by society's corruption. It was like being whisked back to Day One of Creation: "And the earth was formless and void . . . and God said, 'Let there be light'; and there was light; and God saw that the light was good."

They lived in harmony with the earth. The dominion they exercised was benevolent, not cruel. The strict discipline maintained by the Many was hardly despotic. By contrast, they were aware of the way things were, in the "Holy City," ruled by impure priests, ignoble kings, and a selfish soldiery. But they had a clear purpose and a desert vision of the way things ought to be, if only they would all teach by example, and make it so. It all comes down to vision, to the high calling one believes in, and the determination not to allow the things that matter to become adulterated by things that do not. The Sons of Light took into account the need for the whole community to preserve its central perspective and focus, its reason for being.

Earlier in the long history of Judea, a visionary group of "freedom fighters" sought to throw off the yoke of foreign oppressors, a dynasty from Syria that outlawed the faith of Israel and crucified those who refused to abandon their fidelity to the Eternal. They were called by the name "Maccabee," meaning "hammer," because they drove hammer blows into the flanks of Syria's armies. They liberated Jerusalem, cleansed the temple, which the Syrians had defiled, and declared a great feast to celebrate the redemption—Hanukkah. But in time, the noble visionaries who began the revolt lost their way. Their motives turned political, their tactics despotic. Those who threw off the yoke of a foreign king established their own monarchy, just as tyrannical as the one they had deposed. In succeeding, they failed. Their very success corrupted them.

That is why the Sons of Light, whose hearts had remained pure, chose this desert and the lake called Asphaltis. Together they were determined to find the purity their people and their nation had lost. That is why they maintained their sacred rituals—bathing regularly in cold water—to symbolize outwardly the purity they must always manifest inwardly. They never lost their perspective as so many others had. They never succumbed to the universal human malady of adulteration and putrefaction. The prophet of old said it well: "Behold, I am doing a new thing; now it springs forth, do you not perceive it? I will make a way in the wilderness and rivers in the desert . . . to give drink to my chosen people" (Isaiah 43:19–20).

Perspective

The ancient historian writes compellingly of the Essenes' particular methodology for finding focus and attaining vision in their lives:

> *And as for their piety towards God, it is very extraordinary; for before sunrising they speak not a word about profane matters, but put up certain prayers which they have received from their forefathers, as if they made a supplication for its rising.*
> —Josephus, WARS, II, VIII, 5

As modern philosophers have observed, the mind's perception of its own activities, the internal activities of the self, can be changed just by a moment's internal interpretation. Thinking makes it so. That is the key to gaining perspective. The Sons of Light recognized that perspective and simplicity are intimately intertwined. The more things there are to distract you, the more difficult it becomes to cultivate a healthy outlook on life. Simplification is really a matter of arranging priorities. You decide what is important in life, and the rest is dross. Sometimes you have to stop in your tracks, take a deep breath, and bring your material life back into focus. Little wonder that the community of the Essenes had the habit of rising, one and all, well before dawn, offering up prayers and refusing to speak at all about "profane matters."

"Holiness," as they understood it, is really about "separation"—of the inner self from the externals—and preserving the inner self against the whirlwind of stress that twists the soul like a knotted rope. Those who cannot find the internal refuge of the soul by means of this "separation" are ultimately unable to cope with life. But if one can rise early, in the predawn stillness, not to rush about madly in preparation for the day ahead but in utter *separation from* the day ahead, perspective is maintained, no matter what challenges the day may bring.

The lay of the land in the great rift valley is ideally suited to this discipline, for the sheer furnace produced as the sun rises high over the sulfurous lake makes labor outdoors almost impossible from the noon hour on. Work began at dawn, which meant that prayer and meditation commenced in earnest while the early morning stars still shone brightly. Cares and preoccupation could never completely vanish, nor should they. But as the great valley stretches out toward either horizon, masked by the silent heavens, extending toward infinity, one sees the universe and one's place in it with a great deal more clarity. Standing in the desert's mighty open jaw, a member of this ancient order could not help but feel the fragility and transience of life as well as the supreme omnipotence of the Creator. In the great psalter of the community we read:

> *You have envisioned and prepared all things from the beginning of time—to judge and assess all of Your creations even before causing them to exist—an army of angelic spirits, along with a community of righteous ones—the firmament of the*

*heavens and all that they contain—the earth, along with all
of its produce—the oceans in their great depths—according to
all Your plans for all eternity. You determined their existence
before the beginning of time. You have established them from
the foundation of the world. ... You were there before the
beginning and You will have no end.*
—PSALMS SCROLL, col. 5:13–16, 18–19

We wonder how many other Dead Sea psalms were composed in this very stillness:

*As for me, I have been fashioned from mere dust. I was made
from nothing more than clay. I am a source of contamination,
debasement, and corruption. I am a mass of dust, mingled
with water. My dwelling is full of darkness and gloom. I am a
creation of clay, destined to crumble to dust. In time I will return to the dust—to that from which I was fashioned. What
will dust and ashes, such as I, say to the One who made me?
How can dust comprehend the Eternal's works? How can I
stand up straight before the One who censures me—before
perfect holiness, before the eternal spring, before the fountain
of glory, before the well of knowledge?*
—PSALMS SCROLL, col. 20:24–29

The rich imagery of thirsty dust contrasts with the vision
of the spring, the well, and the fountain, and expresses exactly
what the Sons of Light must certainly have experienced on a
daily basis, for they channeled the desert rains from the distant
hills into their pools, their cisterns, and their ritual immersion
baths. They did indeed make rivers in the desert. The tone in
these psalms is not despairing. This is no "desert nihilism" but
a humble acknowledgment of how small we are. It amounts to

a simple affirmation that the universe does not revolve around us. And if we are very small, then how much smaller are the problems and frustrations that so easily take us captive.

In this setting life is no haphazard, chance phenomenon. The ancient historian writes:

> But the sect of the Essenes affirm, that fate governs all things, and that nothing befalls men but what is according to its determination.
>
> —Josephus, ANTIQUITIES, XIII, VI, 9

The Sons of Light took comfort in their conviction that there is without question a rhyme and reason to everything, that all that transpires happens for a greater, unseen purpose and a greater good. Today, faced with scientific disciplines that explain the functioning of the entire cosmos in terms of randomness and entropy, we increasingly look to more metaphysical disciplines to find meaning and purpose.

Life beyond Life

Prevalent among the Sons of Light was an idea shared in ancient Judea by the sect called the Pharisees and another sect called the Nazarenes, or "Christians": resurrection. The Essenes believed that there is life beyond life, that human souls are not destined for oblivion but are immortal. It was an aspect of their perspective that bestowed special strength upon them. This is not an idea to be taken for granted, since many in Judea, such as the vast and powerful Sadducee party, denied the hereafter altogether. But just as many moderns are drawn to accounts of those who have had near-death experiences, the Sons of Light took comfort in the thought that whatever we may suffer in this temporal life is not to be compared with what we shall find in the life to come. The historian observes:

For their doctrine is this: That bodies are corruptible, and that the matter they are made of is not permanent; but that the souls are immortal, and continue for ever; and that they come out of the most subtle air, and are united to their bodies as in prisons, into which they are drawn by a certain natural enticement; but that when they are set free from the bonds of the flesh, they then, as released from a long bondage, rejoice and mount upward. And this is like the opinion of the Greeks, that good souls have their habitations beyond the ocean, in a region that is neither oppressed with storms of rain or snow, nor with intense heat, but that this place is such as is refreshed by the gentle breathing of a west wind, that is perpetually blowing from the ocean . . . which is built first on this supposition, that souls are immortal; and thence are those exhortations to virtue, and dehortations from wickedness collected; whereby good men are bettered in the conduct of their life, by the hope they have of reward after death. . . . These are the divine doctrines of the Essenes about the soul, which lay an unavoidable bait for such as have once had a taste for the philosophy.

— Josephus, WARS, II, VIII, II

Ritual

Notwithstanding their faith in the world to come, the Sons of Light did not speculate about the hereafter at the expense of the present. Life is to be lived, not in the next life but in the eternal now. For this reason their lives were circumscribed by various spiritual disciplines and rituals. Their morning prayers and supplications were part of a much more comprehensive set of rituals, which encompassed the whole of life.

Human life and experience have always been acknowledged with rituals to mark and make sacred such rites of passage as birth, coming of age, marriage, and death. Much of the rich tradition of human ritual has been abandoned in our profoundly secular and technological age, leaving us adrift in an impersonal universe. But there is renewed interest in reclaiming and adopting such traditions, which granted a dignity to the daily routine of life. To this end the Secret Scrolls provide rich examples of ancient sacramental living.

The Sons of Light, in filling their lives with multiple rituals of piety, also increased the acuity of their metaphysical vision. For example, they regularly affixed small boxes containing the central declarations of the Israelite faith to their foreheads and forearms. (This practice, which persists in Orthodox Judaism to the present day, is known as "wrapping *tefillin*.") They constantly read, studied, and copied the sacred texts. They recited a multitude of blessings, even upon their most mundane activities. They immersed themselves daily in ritual baths to symbolize the process of inner spiritual cleansing.

The ultimate function of all this ritual was not for the Sons of Light to separate themselves from the material world but instead that they might bring a metaphysical depth and meaning to "ordinary" life. As philosopher Abraham Joshua Heschel put it, experiencing holiness is really a matter of sanctifying the secular. Moreover, the rituals we perform cause us to pause momentarily during the course of our affairs, to put things back in perspective once again, and to bring a level of sanctity to our actions and behavior.

Meditation

One of the most important rituals among the Sons of Light was the practice of meditation. The precise practice of meditation is deceptively simple. It involves sitting still, adopting the right posture, breathing deeply, letting the heart rate slow, clearing the mind of external concerns, and simply feeling the rhythm of the universe.

But the ancient biblical culture, of which the Sons of Light were a part, understood meditation in a yet broader sense. For them the whole of life became a form of meditation. For in their study, their prayers and blessings, their meticulous copying of the sacred texts, the minutest details of their lives became subject to the meditative purpose. Moreover, the inner fortitude produced by this meditation seems to have released external, miraculous power. As a result of their depth of vision, the Sons of Light were rumored to accomplish the working of miracles, signs, wonders, and divine healings. They were indeed true to their name—the Hebrew/Aramaic word *Osin* (transmuted to "Essene")—"doers" of the works and the will of God.

But not even the Sons of Light were omniscient and all-knowing. One scroll fragment—discovered atop Masada, the rocky plateau not far from the Dead Sea—reads in part:

> *No one, not even among the people who have revealed knowledge, can begin to understand the Eternal's wonders before they are accomplished. When the Eternal does them, not even the doers of righteousness (or "gods") may comprehend them, because they were part of the divine purpose even before they came into being.*
>
> —SONG OF SABBATH SACRIFICES (4Q402), frag. 4, 14–15

In its use of the term "gods," this fascinating passage gives us valuable insight into the high and holy level of their calling. But how was this "revealed knowledge" of which the fragment speaks ultimately to be discerned? Without question, meditation was the key:

> *I will intone and chant Your covenantal love. I will meditate on Your strength and power all through the day. I will always bless Your name, and I will tell of Your glory among the*

children of Adam. My soul will be forever joyful in the abun-
dance of Your goodness.
—PSALMS SCROLL, COL. 19:5–7

Intuition

Judging from many passages in the scrolls and all that we know of them from the historical writings, another spiritual capability exercised by the Sons of Light was a strong sense of intuition. Once they established and oriented their perspective aright, their intuitive senses, including their sense of "vision," was significantly enhanced. Of course, by the time the sect appeared on the scene (in late antiquity), the age of the great prophets—Isaiah, Jeremiah, Ezekiel, and company—had long passed. "Prophecy has ceased!" the contemporary religious leaders declared. The Sons of Light, however, disagreed. They learned a new, uniquely invigorating way of seeing things. They took up the torch of prophecy; they kept alive the conscience of the nation. Of them the ancient historian wrote:

> *Many of these Essenes have, by their excellent virtue, been*
> *thought worthy of the knowledge of divine revelations.*
> —Josephus, ANTIQUITIES, XV, X, 5

> *There are also among them who undertake to foretell things*
> *to come, by reading the holy books, and using several sorts*
> *of purifications, and being perpetually conversant in the*
> *discourses of the prophets; and it is but seldom that they miss*
> *in their predictions.*
> —Josephus, WARS, II, VIII, 12

Call it prophecy; call it prescience, foresight, or being in touch. If the word "prophecy" sounds intimidating or too religious, then call it "intuition." Whatever we call it, this process of listening to one's inner voice is a way of life for some. It involves an acknowledgment that reason and intellect will take us only so far, that the metaphysical universe desperately wants to communicate with the physical realm. If this is so, then prophecy is indeed something that can be learned, cultivated, and developed. The idea really isn't so strange. After all, Albert Einstein noted that we use only about 10 percent of our brains. The other 90 percent is a great reservoir of intuitive power, virtually untapped by most of us.

The Sons of Light believed that prophecy/intuition involves not so much listening for some distant voice from the great beyond as listening to ourselves, to the deep resonance of our own souls. It is a matter of "centering down" to our heart of hearts, to recognize the rich chords of understanding and insight that we knew were there all along. The ancient Israelite sages made repeated reference to a "daughter voice," which they termed a "*Bat Kol,*" and which they hoped would speak to them from the realm of pure Spirit. But somehow, most people who have sought heavenly utterance down through history have realized in the end that the divine voice sounds a great deal like their own.

Many modern scholars of the biblical text prefer to speak of the prophets not as "foretellers" but as "forth-tellers" who would hold forth from the deep well of their souls, thundering the accumulated wealth of their intuition. The biblical prophets, the Sons of Light included, represented a unique troupe, unlike any group of sages the ancient world had ever produced. They weren't soothsayers, astrologers, or black magicians. They were a breed apart from the Babylonian magi or the Delphic oracle. They acted as voices of justice, ethics, and moral conduct. Their commitment to truth was unflinching, and their moral authority was such that kings trembled at their

words. It is an amazing commentary on the times that King
Herod, the mighty potentate of Judea, should honor the Essenes among all his subjects (whom he generally despised) not
because they possessed weaponry or political influence or liai-
son with foreign powers, but because they were prophets:

> *Now there was one of these Essenes, whose name was*
> *Menahem, who had the foreknowledge of future events given*
> *him by God. This man once saw Herod when he was a child,*
> *going to school, and saluted him as king of the Jews. Menahem*
> *clapped him on his backside with his hand, and said, "You shall*
> *be king, and shall begin your reign happily. ... " Now at that*
> *time Herod paid no attention to what Menahem said, as having*
> *no hopes of such advancement; but a little afterward, when he*
> *was so fortunate as to be advanced to the dignity of king, and*
> *was in the height of his dominion, he sent for Menahem, and*
> *asked him how long he should reign. He replied, "Twenty, no,*
> *thirty years!" Herod was satisfied with these replies, and gave*
> *Menahem his hand, and from that time he continued to honor*
> *all the Essenes. Many of these Essenes have, by their excellent*
> *virtue, been thought worthy of this knowledge of divine revela-*
> *tions. Herod ... continued to honor all the Essenes.*
>
> —Josephus, ANTIQUITIES, XV, X, 5

But how does one cultivate such a keen sense of intuition?
The Sons of Light would explain that prophetic gifts are merely
adjuncts: Of purity of soul and body. Of living uprightly, and
above all simply. Of telling the truth at all times. Of being honest
and forthright, admitting mistakes and accepting chastisement.
Of rising early and meditating. Of perceiving one's essential
union with nature and with the eternal cosmos. Of saying little
and doing much. Of listening more than speaking. Of caring
about others more than oneself. Then, in the inner sanctum of

the soul, you hear a voice that resonates with your own, like an echo from the chalky cliffs, full of insight, rich with knowledge, pregnant with purpose. The Sons of Light would counsel to let that voice change and reorder your own life first, leading you into deeper commitment and purpose Then, slowly, be open to sharing the hidden wisdom of that voice with those around you.

Apocalypse

The world has changed more in the last century than in all previous centuries put together. More people are alive today than in all previous ages put together, and the earth's resources are strained. The Sons of Light, in their day, were preparing for difficult times ahead—for an impending apocalypse. Their words of warning sound hauntingly like those of many modern "prophets" who claim that the world cannot go on much longer. Apocalyptists have always been around, and countless prophecies of gloom and doom and deadlines for the end of the world have slipped by unfulfilled. The Essenes are an example of people who sincerely believed that the end was near—any day—and that those who have knowledge had better be prepared. Yet, in spite of their reputation for great accuracy in their predictions, the sect was destined to disappear; and still the end did not come. . . .

The Essenes believed that the whole world might well become an empty wasteland, as barren as the desert of Judea, if the behavior of the "Sons of Darkness" brought about divine retribution. A great apocalyptic scroll found among the Dead Sea library is called the *War Scroll*. It depicts, in a prophetic way, great conflict between the forces of good (the Sons of Light) and the forces of evil (the Sons of Darkness) at the end of the age.

For all the attention devoted to it, there is, however, one aspect of the *War Scroll* that is seldom noticed. While a series of fierce battles are predicted, the battles themselves are not actually described. Instead, the bulk of the document is a vivid description of liturgical praise. At the heart of it there is no fighting at all, but participation in a great liturgical ceremony, with trumpets, standards, and shining armor. In the final analysis, the battle is won by praise, by personal purity, by a noble state of mind.

Desert Messiahs

One additional hallmark of the faith of the Sons of Light was the profound belief that history is going somewhere, that this present broken world will be redeemed one day by an anointed one, a messiah—or more properly, two messiahs—who will accomplish a mighty repair of the whole planet. Traditionally Judaism has acknowledged a single messianic figure. The Essenes, believing in two such figures, therefore represent a starkly disparate version of Jewish messianism. Never-theless, the idea of a messiah, an anointed one—who will come one day to repair the broken world, who will bring about a messianic age, wherein war will be abolished, the lion will lie down with the lamb, and swords will be beaten into plowshares—is one of the most intoxicating concepts ever to have come forth among the human family. The very word "messiah" refers to an anointing, which in turn implies a kingship, a divine right to bring about a just and holy rule upon the earth. But the Sons of Light did not sit still while waiting for the messianic age to dawn. Their work was to bring forth the messianic age. The groundwork having been accomplished by the Sons of Light, the Secret Scroll known as the *Midrash on the Last Days* goes on to describe the work of the messiahs to come:

> *He is the Branch of David. He will rise up, along with the*
> *Interpreter of the Law, who will govern Zion in the end of*

days. For it is written (in Amos 9:11), "I will restore the Tent of David, which has fallen." Interpreted, this means that the fallen Tent of David is the one who will rise up to bring salvation to Israel.

—4QFLORILEGIUM, 11–13

Two messiahs are clearly referenced here. The sacred text announces the coming of a "Branch of David" (an anointed ruler from the lineage of King David) as well as an "Interpreter of the Law" (a priestly messiah and member of the tribe of Levi). Both shall be required to raise the fallen "tent of David."

Long ago, a great tabernacle stood in the desert, a "tent of witness," which served as a repository for the Ten Commandments, written on tablets of stone and placed within a golden Ark of the Covenant. Behind lofty curtains, in a place called the Holy of Holies, the Ark rested. Over this great tabernacle hovered a pillar of cloud by day and a pillar of fire by night, evincing the awesome presence of the Almighty. The Sons of Light certainly held to this fundamental vision. The image of the Divine Presence, hovering upon and permeating the entire community, kept and sustained them. And yet something had gone awry with this splendid vision. The tent of David had fallen. The Divine Presence seemed to have departed. That is why the Sons of Light came to the desert—to raise up the tabernacle anew, to lead by example, to establish a new community, wherein the Divine Presence would be pleased to dwell. An amazing passage catches the spirit of this vision:

Please remember that we are Your people. You are the One who carried us wonderfully on eagle's wings. You have brought us to Yourself. You are like an eagle that vigilantly watches over its nest and its little ones, hovering about them. You have spread out Your wings, taking one at a time and carrying it on Your pinions.

Therefore, we dwell alone, separated from the rest. We are not
considered among the other nations. Yet, You are among us,
dwelling in the pillar of fire and in the cloud of Your splendor. You
continually walk ahead of us, and Your glory travels in our midst.
—THE WORDS OF THE HEAVENLY LIGHTS (4Q504), frag. 6:6–11

Desert Dreams

Living with vision is about more than just living life rea-
sonably and responsibly, shouldering one's burdens, and performing expected tasks. People often confuse such attributes
with true leadership. The "vision thing" is equally about
dreaming, about seeing things while wide awake that most
people see only in their sleep.

As Jonathan Swift once observed, "Vision is the art of seeing things invisible." All of us need sleep, just as we need food,
water, and oxygen. Deprive a person of sleep for a night or two,
and the senses are greatly impaired, to the point that the individual can barely function. Deprive a person of sleep for a
longer period of time, even for a few consecutive nights, and
near-madness results, including wild hallucinations and de-
ranged fantasies. A case can in fact be made that it is not so
much sleep that a living being needs but dreams—the deep,
"REM" kind of sleep that allows the unconscious mind to wan-
der where it will. Human beings are dreamers by nature, and to
short-circuit the dream factory of our minds is to diminish our
very humanness. For without dreams, we truly have no vision.
Thoreau claimed that "Dreams are the touchstones of our character." Little wonder that the Secret Scrolls are so frequently devoted to the seeing of visions and the dreaming of dreams.

In one very important fragment, the so-called *Visions of
Amram*, we find a powerful "dream-vision" describing the illumination of the Sons of Light and the black gloom of the Sons

of Darkness. We also find a mystical encounter with a host of angelic "watchers," who survey the whole earth, revealing the purpose and the goal toward which history is headed—of which the Essenes are an integral part:

> *In my vision I had a glimpse of the heavenly Watchers. Two of them were engaged in a heated argument about me. I asked them, "Who are you?" ... They answered me, saying, "We are the ones who govern the sons of Adam. ... For all the Sons of Light will gleam with luminescence; but all the Sons of Darkness will be dim with gloom. ... Indeed, all fools and evil people will be dark; but the wise and the truthful will radiate light. The Sons of Light go toward the light—toward unending delight and rapture. ... For the people will be bathed with light.*
> —VISIONS OF AMRAM (4Q544), frag. 1:10–12; (4Q548), frag. 1:9–13

Vision, according to the scrolls, is what gives light, what enables us to see, regardless of physical sight, or the lack of vision of our foes. This is why we must dream—to catch a sense of vision beyond ourselves—to authenticate our existence as part of a greater purpose in perfecting the world.

If You Will It, It Is Not a Dream

A more modern example of the power of the vision and the dream may be found in the life of a certain journalist for a Viennese periodical, an assimilated Austrian Jew assigned to cover a case of espionage in France. His name was Theodore Herzl—a comely gentleman with a dark beard, thick black hair, and the piercing eyes of a dreamer. On trial in Paris was a French military officer, Captain Alfred Dreyfus, who had been accused of the crime of espionage, for allegedly passing a French artillery manual to a German military attaché. The trial was sensational, and Herzl the journalist initially believed, as did the mass of the French citizenry, that Dreyfus was guilty. But in time Herzl came to realize that public sentiment was being motivated by another stark fact—that Captain Dreyfus happened to be a Jew. When Herzl began hearing cries of "Death to Jews!" in the streets, he decided that the Dreyfus affair amounted to nothing more than an anti-Semitic show-trial. It represented the desire of the great majority of the French people to damn one Jew and, through him, all Jews. The Viennese journalist who, prior to this time, was barely in touch with his own Jewish heritage, transformed himself into a firebrand for justice, seeking the complete exoneration of Dreyfus.

Justice was not easily to be served, however, and Dreyfus, far from being vindicated, was instead sentenced to hard labor on Devil's Island, off the coast of French Guiana. For Theodore Herzl, the sad events inaugurated a personal vision—the dream to reestablish, after two long millennia, an independent Jewish nation on the shores of Palestine. Through the efforts of a single man and his impossible dream, Zionism was born.

The task would not be easy. The ancient land of Israel, including the area once inhabited by the Sons of Light, lay in lonely desolation, having been alternately neglected and raped by century upon century of unmerciful occupiers. The proud forests of antiquity were gone, and in their place were disease-ridden malarial swamps. In those days a crumbling outpost of the rotting Ottoman Empire, Palestine was anything but desirable turf. Herzl wrote, "Perhaps these ideas are not practical ones at all and I am only making myself the laughingstock of the people to whom I talk about it seriously." [12] But in spite of persistent doubts, the dream would rule the day. When all was said and done, "reality," for Herzl the visionary, counted for little. He therefore began writing a proposed "blueprint" for a hypothetical homeland for his people in Palestine. He called it

Der Judenstaat—The Jewish State. In his vision, published in Vienna in 1896, he saw a new Israel, its inhabitants living securely in a reclaimed, replanted land, ancient yet fully modern. It would be an exemplary state, a light to the nations, and, like the Sons of Light of so long ago, it would hold a moral compass for humanity.

Herzl embarked on a lecture tour to build support for his radical ideas. Making his way from Berlin to Munich to Vienna to Paris to London, he preached his message of redemption. In Bulgaria enthusiastic Jews went so far as to hail him as the Messiah, the "anointed one," who would at last bring deliverance to his scattered people. In his personal journal, he referred to the Zionist vision as "a work of infinite grandeur . . . a mighty dream."[13] In 1897 in Basel, Switzerland, he organized the first of a series of international Zionist congresses. Theory had to be matched with practical measures. Herzl approached the Ottoman Turks, offering to buy Palestine on behalf of the Jewish people. The Ottomans, not wishing a "foreign" entity to arise on the edges of their crumbling empire, adamantly refused to sell. Undaunted, Herzl proceeded to talk to the British, who owned half of the world and who just might be persuaded to cede one of their possessions to the Jewish people. The British proposed the sale of Uganda, in east Africa. Desperate to secure at least some territory for the Jewish state, Herzl presented the idea to the Zionist Congress, which, after considerable debate, turned it down. It had to be Palestine.

Theodore Herzl would not give up, however. His vision was audacious enough to inspire his people, who had been downtrodden and persecuted for centuries. In 1902 he published a visionary novel, depicting the inhospitable terrain of Palestine as viewed by both a Jew and a gentile, who happened to be traveling to a far-off island. These same traveling companions are depicted again, a few decades later, viewing the land after it has undergone a major metamorphosis, becoming a Jewish state. Herzl called his book *Das Altneuland* (*The Old New Land*), which is exactly what it was. For an ancient yet modern people have made the desert bloom, cooperatively transforming Palestine into a verdant realm of farms linked by canals, new roads, sparkling cities and towns, lighted by night through the miracle of electricity, and blessed by every modern amenity. The Old City of Jerusalem has been repaved with fresh stone, cleaned, and tidied up. There are new parks, broad, tree-lined avenues, shops, and schools. Ancient Jericho has become a winter resort. In Herzl's novel, Jews and Arabs live together in harmony.

A single axiom, representing the book's thematic message, became a catchphrase, not only of the book, but of Theodore Herzl's life's work: "If you will it, it is not a dream." His point was that dreams require will, in order to be clothed in reality. In his conclusion Herzl added, "Dream and action are not so far apart as is often thought. All the acts of mankind were dreams once and will become dreams again."

Theodore Herzl never saw his dreams come to fruition. Decades, and the horrific experience of the Holocaust, would pass before the state of Israel was born. But Herzl's vision would long outlive him, and the "Father of Zionism" today lies buried on the western outskirts of modern Jerusalem, near a broad, tree-lined avenue, like those described in his novel.

What Dreams May Come

The Sons of Light had their own visionary blueprint, describing a redeemed Israel and a new Jerusalem. It is called the *Temple Scroll,* known for being the longest of all the texts in the Dead Sea library. The Essenes wrote it because in their eyes, the entire priesthood (and the Temple with it) had become corrupt, fat with opulence, and caring nothing for the spiritual ideals they cherished. Since the Temple had been defiled, the sacrifices and offerings had become empty and meaningless. There must be a superior way, a vision of something better.

This is what the *Temple Scroll* represents—the dream of a new spiritual center in the heart of Jerusalem, beaming light to all the world yet existing, for the time being, only in your minds. The Eternal has spoken, as follows:

> *I will live among you forever. I will sanctify my Temple with My glory. . . .*
> *You are to fashion stairways in the house you are to build. You are to construct a building housing a great stairway on the north side of the Temple. . . .*
> *You are to make a gate, opening to the roof of the Sanctuary, in the upper storey of this building. . . .*
> *You are to cover this entire building with gold—including the walls, the gates, and the roof, both inside and out—as well as the pillar and the steps ascending to it. You are to do exactly as I tell you. . . .*
> *I want you to sanctify everything in the vicinity of the altar, as well as the Sanctuary, the Laver, and the porch of pillars. All of these things will be in a state of utmost holiness, world without end!*
>
> —TEMPLE SCROLL, col. 29:7–8; 30:3–5; 31:6–9; 35:8–9

As the scroll unfolds its vision, everything is represented in detail—the precise dimensions of the monumental edifice, the nature of the sacrifices to be offered up upon the altar, additional pillared courtyards and chambers, and enormous gates of symbolic meaning. Everything is to be made according to the supernatural pattern revealed from on high. The visionary edifice and its vast courtyards were never to be constructed, for the Sons of Light were destined to disappear mysteriously before the blueprint could be clothed in reality. But the vision and the dream embodied in the scroll doubtless energized the brave little sect, bestowing upon them a transcendental purpose that kept them alive for two long centuries. One thing is abundantly clear: Dreams never really die; they are only transmuted and reincarnated, from one form to another, from generation to generation.

Modern Israel, Theodore Herzl's Israel, still waits for the day in which the great Temple will be erected, rebuilt upon the very site where Abraham was said to have offered up his son Isaac. Perhaps someday it shall be built, just as the Sons of Light have ordained.

4 Labor:
Conquest of the Self

IF THOU WORKEST AT THAT WHICH IS
before thee, following right reason seri-
ously, vigorously, calmly, without allow-
ing anything else to distract thee, but
keeping thy divine part pure, as if thou
art bound to give it back immediately; if
thou holdest to this, expecting nothing,
fearing nothing, but satisfied with thy
present activity . . . thou wilt live happy.

—Marcus Aurelius,
MEDITATIONS, Book III, 12

F ROM WHAT we know from the scrolls themselves, the re-
marks of the historian Josephus about the Essenes, and
the archaeology of the settlement of Qumran, we can
imagine what a day in the life of the ancient sect must have
been like.

The day is still young when the Sons of Light set their
hands to work. There is no time to waste, for all too soon the
stifling heat of the desert will make labor unbearable. They
must focus their minds early, resolving inwardly to accomplish

the tasks set before them. The members of this desert sect have no dread of hard work. On the contrary, they relish the opportunity to labor, for in their work they are doing as the ancient prophet Isaiah commanded. They are making a way in the wilderness, forging a path for the Many, the community of the redeemed. The struggle of their hands is full of holy purpose. As the Secret Scrolls maintain:

> *This is the appointed time—for preparing the Way into the wilderness!*
> —MANUAL OF DISCIPLINE, col. 9:19–20

They work not for some foreign taskmaster but as a cohesive whole.

Of Ants and Men

The morning ritual, of course, begins with prayer and meditation. It is written:

> *After this every one of them are sent away by their curators, to exercise some of those arts wherein they are skilled, in which they labor with great diligence till the fifth hour. After which they assemble themselves together again into one place; and when they have clothed themselves in white veils they then bathe their bodies in cold water.*
> —Josephus, WARS, II, VIII, 5

Like worker ants moving dust and earth with singleness of purpose to build the nest, the Sons of Light till the soil, tend to the crops, and participate in the maintenance of the settlement. Each individual has a stake in the success of the whole.

The work is highly diversified, and each person is assigned specific duties. When those duties are carried out the entire operation proceeds smoothly. As with the ants, there is no compulsion, dread, or fear. The Sons of Light work hard because they want to. After all, there are no other options. Life is labor and labor is life. The unity they already sense with the cosmos is enhanced as the seeds they plant sprout from the earth. But the fields must be irrigated in this barren wasteland, or all will return to dust. An elaborate system of aqueducts, which have been carved into the rocky terrain, extend from the canyon floor up the slope of the chalky hills in the distance, channeling water directly into cisterns and, in turn, into the fields. The symmetry of labor is a reflection of the symmetry of creation, and the individual's place in it is never compromised.

The members of the community take pride in what they produce by the sweat of their brow. But theirs is not an individual pride that seeks betterment at the expense of others. For as with the ants, prosperity is not a personal thing but a communal accomplishment. Their own labors are, by themselves, insignificant. The true reward—far more than food, shelter, and clothing—is a fellowship shared with their neighbors. Since the fruit of labor is enjoyed by the Many, the labor itself is experienced by the whole community. In other words, labor has no selfish ends. Consequently, in their labor, they are neither lorded over nor do they lord it over others.

From farming, to cooking, to building, to plastering, to the copying of sacred scrolls, there is no letup in the incessant rhythm of tasks to be accomplished. Of the sect it is reported:

> *They think to be sweaty is a good thing, as they do also to be clothed in white garments.*
> —Josephus, WARS, II, VIII, 3

Indeed, there is nothing wrong with sweat, and this admonition is taken to heart, as each bears his neighbor's burdens with patience and forbearance. There is great dignity in this labor (hence, the white garments), for each Son of Light sees in the faces of his comrades the tangible fruit of his exertion.

As midday blazes all around, the perspiration pours from each brow. Just as they have risen early, their physical labor must end early, for no one can work long in these conditions. The "fifth hour" brings them back to the massive buildings of the settlement, retiring to the relative cool of the limestone quarters. One after another, the Sons of Light submerge themselves in a *mikveh*, a plaster-covered ritual immersion bath, to attain a measure of religious purity. Thus their labor, which began in meditation, ends in primal innocence, sealing it with high and holy purpose.

Scribes of Light

In a similar spirit of awe other members of the community have been engaged all day in the most important work of all: the copying of their sacred texts. It is a monumental effort, and embarking upon it must have required the support and dedication of the entire community. Certainly many members must have been directly involved in the endeavor. While some have worked to plant and to harvest, others have devoted themselves to the scribal arts. A huge room of the settlement has been set aside for this purpose. Selected Sons of Light gather in small groups, freshly bathed and dressed in their finest white garments, huddling over long plaster tables, spending many hours each day copying the contents of one scroll onto another. The methods used in producing scrolls have remained unchanged for thousands of years, and those who labor today to copy the books of the Hebrew Bible generally employ the same techniques as the scribes of antiquity. The steps followed by contemporary scribes—as well as their ancient counterparts—are multiple. The skins of kosher animals must first be prepared. Having been carefully removed from the carcass, all remaining fat and hairs are scrubbed away. They are then cut into long, rectangular sheets, suitable for writing. Each resulting sheet, called a *klaf,* is ready to be sewed into a larger parchment—a scroll.

Before writing can commence, each *klaf* has to be scored, with the very faintest of black lines, from which the Hebrew letters are hung. Hebrew is written from right to left, and the letters descend from the lines rather than sitting on top of them. The ink is also of a special formula, a mixture of galnut (the bump on a tree bark where a wasp has stung it to lay its eggs), carbon powder, copper sulfate crystals, and gum arabic (tree sap, to make it stick to the parchment). Those who serve as scribes dab their quills into ceramic inkwells, but cannot press quill to parchment without reciting or chanting each word they write. The "scriptorium" at the Dead Sea settlement must have been abuzz every day with the sound of scribes, chanting each word, each letter, as one word flowed into the next.

During the course of writing, whenever one of the scribes comes upon the sacred, divine name of God (YHWH—יהוה), he must put down his quill, head off to the *mikveh,* and dip himself in cold water to attain a higher degree of ritual purity. Returning to the scriptorium, he cannot pick up the same quill. He must choose a fresh one and dip it in a special well of ink, reserved only for writing the divine name. Furthermore, he does not write the sacred name with the same Hebrew letters he uses for the rest of the text. Instead, he writes it using an earlier form of the alphabet, employed at the time of King David, so as to set it apart as particularly holy.

The process of producing a scroll is excruciating. It takes many months to transcribe a single document. Furthermore, there are many documents to copy, including thirty-eight books of the Hebrew Bible—the Law of Moses, the Prophets, and the "Wisdom Books," Psalms, Proverbs, and the like. There are also original epic works (considered by modern scholars to be of Essene composition), such as the *Manual of Discipline,* the *War Scroll,* the Essene *Psalms,* the *Temple Scroll,* the *Damascus Rule,* and many others.

When it comes to the host of biblical and apocryphal books among the Dead Sea library, the scribes clearly copied from yet older texts, none of which have survived to the present day. Consequently, the Dead Sea Scrolls represent the oldest copies of the Hebrew Bible known in the world. While there are some minor variations among these versions of the Bible, they are nonetheless remarkably similar to what later became the canonical text of the scriptures. It is clear, however, that other books, including manuals and rule books as well as psalms, prophesies and visions, and assorted narratives, were original compositions of the Essenes. Some of them were undergoing continual revision, as evidenced by disparate versions of the same text found among the caves. Some of these may have been composed orally and copied from memory.

Moderns often wonder why a community would go to such painstaking trouble to copy a library of works by hand, when simply staying alive in the desert was such a challenge. The answer is that the Sons of Light would likely have perished quickly had they not devoted themselves to the scribal arts. We human beings have a very hard time living, growing, building, or being the least bit happy, unless we measure it all by being connected, not only to others but also to a goal and purpose larger than ourselves. Whatever societies anthropologists study, however "primitive," the same features are always there—a belief in something beyond this world, multiple rituals to sharpen that belief, and some sort of textual tradition, written or oral, by which to transmit that belief. It is a universal principle, and moderns who ignore it, who consider themselves too sophisticated for such "primitive" things, only diminish themselves.

Boundaries

By their labors the Sons of Light established "boundaries" of camaraderie for the whole group. All children want boundaries, say the experts. They want structure and rules. Occasionally, young people join religious orders, sects, or even street gangs, not because doing so is easy but precisely because it is hard. The Sons of Light had the idea that the ancient traditions and customs of the Israelites were being violated, swept away by a "Wicked Priest," a "scoffer," who had sought to replace the rigor of the ancient faith with "smooth things":

> *The Scoffer . . . enticed them to go astray, into a desolate wasteland where there are no paths. He caused the everlasting heights to sink into the abyss. He led the people away from the pathways of justice. He removed the Boundary, used by our ancestors to designate their inheritance.*
> —DAMASCUS RULE, col. 1:14–16

When things are made too easy, people lose their way. The "boundary" that keeps people secure, safe, and distinct is violated. Any societal group whose membership is too easily attained will be little valued. The community rule book spells out the rigor of this way and the labor it will entail:

> FOR THE OVERSEER. . . .
> *The holy ones will be taught to live according to the community rule book. They are to seek the Eternal with all their hearts and all their souls. They are to do what is good and behave with integrity before the Eternal, as was commanded through the hand*

of Moses and through all the prophets—servants of the Eternal.
They are to love all the things which the Eternal has chosen and
to hate all the things which the Eternal has rejected. They are to
keep far away from all evil and cling firmly to what is good.
They are to be truthful and upright in all their dealings, and they
are to cultivate sound judgment upon the earth. They are not to
walk any longer after a corrupt and guilty heart, following lust-
ing eyes and perpetrating all sorts of evil.

   The Eternal will usher into the Covenant of Lovingkindness
all those who freely volunteer themselves to fulfill the holy com-
mandments. They will be brought into the counsel of the
Eternal, walking in simple perfection. This will be in accordance
with everything that has been revealed concerning the predeter-
mined times.

—MANUAL OF DISCIPLINE, col. 1:1–9

Make it hard! That is what the Sons of Light counseled. If
you want someone to follow you, you should not tell them
how easy it will be; you should spell out the cost. Let the value
of your way be confirmed by your labor:

You have established in me the foundation of truth—deep
within my heart. You have offered the waters of the Covenant
for those who are seekers.

—PSALMS SCROLL, col. 13:9

Thomas Paine said, "What we obtain too cheap we esteem
too lightly." John F. Kennedy, in one of the most powerful
speeches of his presidency, stood up to dedicate the resources
of the nation to reaching the moon. Linking this monumental
labor with the other work that needed to be done, he declared,
in words that would galvanize the culture toward doing the
"impossible": "We choose to go to the moon in this decade,

and do the other things, not because they are easy, but because they are hard!" Kennedy understood the psychology of challenge, and he used it to perfect his leadership, to steer the nation on a sure course, to bestow great meaning and value upon the work of teeming millions, to create a vision of "Camelot."

Taming Eden

The desert settlement on the shore of Lake Asphaltis was a most unusual sort of "Camelot"—or Eden. And taming it was no easy task. It was, nonetheless, a holy task, the continuity of the seasons being reflected in the continuity of labor:

> ... the season of harvesting up until the season of summer; the season of sowing up until the season of grasses; the seasons of the years up until the periods of seven years; the beginning of the seven-year periods up until the season of freedom and deliverance. For all of my life the holy ordinances will be engraved on my tongue.
>
> —MANUAL OF DISCIPLINE, col. 10:7–8

The question is, what makes some work seem like tedious drudgery, while other work seems deeply rewarding and fulfilling? How can more of us find the fulfillment and contentment that seemed to pervade the desert society of the Sons of Light?

Trite as it may sound, purpose is essential to all labor. No matter what the financial reward, no matter what measure of prestige a career may promise, it must serve some higher goal. It must in some way have the potential of making the world a better place. Every individual must ask, quite simply: What was I put on this planet to do? When that question is answered, then labor takes on an entirely new light.

Those who wrote the Secret Scrolls had no trouble with this question. They not only tamed their personal desert; they made it bloom. They did it by putting away all distraction, by keeping their purpose at all times "front and center."

The Labor Theory of Value

In contrast to the experience of the Sons of Light, labor and attitudes toward labor provoke more consummate unhappiness than any other malady contemporary society has to cope with. Studies have shown that—in spite of the relative prosperity that prevails in the general culture, in spite of an economic boom of unparalleled longevity, and in spite of disposable income at unheard-of levels—the great majority of modern laborers are profoundly dissatisfied with their working lives. Instead of the phenomenon of the "midlife crisis," one study exposes a "young-life crisis," wherein record numbers of youthful workers are burning out on the fast track and choosing different, less stressful careers. There is a definite trend, declares the study, toward working "for the fun of it." Another study has even turned up evidence that income and job satisfaction may be inversely related. Oddly, not only does money not buy happiness but it also sometimes brings on misery.

To be like a Son of Light, however, involves adopting an attitude toward labor far removed from the prevailing cultural winds. At the heart of this attitude, you are to liberate your labor from selfish ends. You must banish the idea that you work for your own sake, to build your own future, to amass wealth, to advance your status in society. Such ends, while they sound worthy enough, produce neither peace nor contentment but misery. Those who engage in labor for selfish ends do so at their own peril, often finding themselves utterly disconnected from the things that lend meaning and value to labor. Roman philosopher-emperor Marcus Aurelius wrote:

> *For those too are triflers who have wearied themselves in life by their activity, and yet have no object to which to direct every movement, and, in a word, all their thoughts.*
> —Marcus Aurelius, MEDITATIONS, Book II, 7

Or, as stated succinctly in the Dead Sea Psalms:

> *Emptiness and vanity mount upward, even up to the stars!*
> —PSALMS SCROLL, col. 2:27–28

Karl Marx theorized that the value of goods produced derives solely from the labor that went into their production; this is called the "labor theory of value." But the Sons of Light looked at things through different eyes. For them, labor itself had value. If work is wasted on oneself and on the accumulation of things in order to satisfy the ego, its value is lost, for things in themselves have no value. But if you labor on behalf of others, if your work is accomplished with the good of family, friends, and community in mind, if your energy is expended in pursuit of a goal infinitely larger than yourself, you shall labor with meaning and purpose and, ultimately, great joy.

There can and should be joy in labor, and everyone in contemporary society who is not finding such joy should seriously reevaluate either their careers or their attitudes toward their careers. Discover afresh not just the value of labor but also the "values"—the transcendental purpose—of labor. The Secret Scrolls declare:

> *This is the appointed time—for preparing the Way into the wilderness! [The Overseer] will train them in everything that*

will be needed during that time. For this purpose they will be
separated from the company of all people who have not
diverged their way from the path of iniquity.
—MANUAL OF DISCIPLINE, col. 9:19–21

What is this "preparation of the way"? It is two-pronged: internal (attuning the heart and inclining the soul) and external (physically constructing a living settlement in a land of death).

David Ben-Gurion, first prime minister of the modern state of Israel, understood this ancient principle. When he retired at the end of a long political career, he did not choose the lazy anonymity of apartment life in a city (such as Jerusalem or Tel Aviv), but chose instead to live and labor on a rural agricultural co-op, Kibbutz Sde Boker, far to the south, in the Negev Desert. Retirement was inimical for Ben-Gurion. Labor lent value to his very existence. When he grabbed a pitchfork and went out to pitch hay, he was authenticating himself, finding connectedness with the larger community. This same Ben-Gurion, as a tottering old man, would later perch himself on a sand-covered plateau near the kibbutz and by the sweat of his brow would lay the cornerstone for the proposed College of the Negev. This, in his visionary mind, would not just be another university; it would be a "combined Oxford and M.I.T." —a key institution for dispensing light to the world. Of course a man of his stature had no need to labor at all, but the vision of his life demanded it. Ben-Gurion always had a cause greater than himself in which to invest his energies. Without labor he could find no meaning, no purpose, no value.

The nature of Ben-Gurion's labor out in the wilderness must have been quite similar to what the Sons of Light experienced as they dug channels across the canyons to irrigate their fields, as they planted trees in the arid ground, as they carved caves for their dwelling places into the limestone cliffs, as day by day they inscribed their sacred parchments. The Secret Scrolls describe their toil, as though the Eternal One were doing the work on their behalf:

> *By the work of my hand You have opened their wellspring—along with channels of water—turning each channel in the proper direction and planting their trees according to the sun's perfect plumb-line. In the end their branches will be laden with glory. When I extend my hand, digging ditches for the trees, their roots penetrate the solid rock. Their trunks are deeply rooted in the earth. Even in the heat of summer, they remain strong.*
> —PSALMS SCROLL, col. 16:21–24

The success of their labors depended on their diligence, and without their toil, the fragile ecosystem they had introduced to the desert would wither and die. There was a partnership among them, the Eternal, and the land itself. They could see, day by day, the life that their labor yielded. There was eternal meaning and value to every turn of their spades. By their hands the desert bloomed, and without their labor, all would return to dust, reclaimed by the saline landscape round about Lake Asphaltis:

> *But if I pull back my hand, all will become like desert acacia bushes. The trunks will be like nettles in the plains of salt. Only thorns and reeds will grow from the ditches. There will only be brambles and thistles. The trees along the banks will turn into sour vines. All the leaves will wither under the intense heat. None of the stems will reach the spring water.*
> —PSALMS SCROLL, col. 16:24–26

There can be no question about the value of their labor, and nothing but pride to be taken in the daily work of their hands. This solemn partnership is expressed in yet another Dead Sea psalm:

> *You fashioned the spirit of Adam upon the earth, to exercise dominion for all of eternity and for all generations. You have parceled out specific tasks to be accomplished during every generation. All will proceed according to the rules ordained from generation to generation.*
>
> —PSALMS SCROLL, col. 9:15–17

In other words, part of being human comes in performing the "tasks" allotted to you. These tasks link you, across time, with every generation that has gone before. In this your toil is lifted from the mundane and transmuted into an expression of the divine order. You are performing the "works" of the Eternal's hands.

Labor and the Art of War

There is, of course, much more to labor than merely digging ditches and watching the trees and plants take root and blossom. Indeed, the greater part of work is not the effort itself but one's attitude toward one's effort. For even the most odious of tasks can take on richness, depth, and transcendental value when approached with a perspective of dedication, determination, and resolve.

The concepts elaborated by the Sons of Light are found in many societies, in disparate places and across the plane of history. It is especially intriguing, however, to find more or less "direct" influence from the Essenes upon neighboring societies, who carried on Essene ideas long past the denouement of the desert sect itself. While the society of the Essenes became extinct in the late first century of the Common Era, scholars believe that many of the ideas embodied in the sect (including their own version of the "work ethic") were somehow transmitted, perhaps via copies of the scrolls themselves, far to the east-southeast, into the Arabian Desert. There the sacred teachings were picked up by a new and somewhat different expression of the monotheism of the Sons of Light—Islam.

As the story unfolds, a young man named Muhammad in the Arabian city of Mecca was in need of employment. His uncle, Abu Talib, said to him, "I am, as you know, a man of scanty means, and truly the times are hard. Now there is a caravan of your own tribe about to start for Syria, and Khadijah, daughter of Khuwaylid, is in need of the services of men of our tribe to take care of her merchandise. If you offer yourself for the enterprise, she would readily accept it." Muhammad replied, "Be it as you say."[14] Thus began the young prophet's material labors, which would prepare him for the spiritual revelation he was to transmit to the world. Over time, Muhammad's civility, moral probity, and dedication to his work merited the admiration of the forty-year-old, widowed Khadijah. Muhammad, who was only twenty-five, so touched her by his attitude that she proposed marriage to him. Muhammad consented. His life of labor involved character building and personal preparation for the revelation of monotheism that one day would be given to the young prophet.

It was all predestined. What followed—the sudden explosion of a new faith, stressing hard work and discipline in the service of a single God—is nothing short of amazing. Did the earliest Muslims somehow gain access to the Secret Scrolls of the Judean wilderness? Or were the ideas in the scrolls in some way transmitted from ancient Judea into the Arabian Desert, where they were picked up by the culture that spawned Islam?

Whatever the conclusion, the similarities between the Dead Sea Scrolls and the writings of Islam are inescapable.

Among the values of Islam is a conviction near and dear to the ancient Essenes: submission to the perfect will of the Eternal, known in Arabic as Allah. This "submission" (which is what the word "Islam" means) involves a very great measure of discipline, both internal and external. It involves a serious commitment to the principles of labor. One of the most frequently used (yet also one of the most misunderstood) words in Islamic culture is the word *jihad,* very poorly translated as "holy war." The true meaning of the word is "striving in God's path," an exertion that reveals itself in two different ways. There is the "lesser jihad," a physical struggle against external aggression, which may manifest itself in genuine warfare. But there is also the "greater jihad," in which one strives with one's own soul to acquire true spirituality. *Jihad* is best expressed by an individual battle to right wrongs, support goodness, and subdue one's evil inclinations.

Doubtless, the greater struggle is the internal one. As the prophet declared:

> *The most excellent jihad is that for the conquest of the self.*
> —MUHAMMAD

Work means exertion, which Islam understood in the abstract as a type of war. Therefore, whenever you approach a day of labor, you must battle yourself—and every inclination toward sloth and laziness—in order to be productive, to be disciplined, and to find meaning in the tasks of life.

The Sons of Light devoted an entire scroll to the subject of battle: the *War Scroll.* Normally read as a declaration of war against the forces of evil, its implications for the inner life of the individual are rarely grasped. For the *War Scroll* is not only about eschatological conflict at the end of the age; it is also about what Muslims would call the "greater jihad"—an inner struggle that transforms your character, causing you to labor in confronting your assorted inner demons and emerge victorious:

> *Make yourselves strong and full of courage. Become true war-*
> *riors. Do not let yourselves become fearful. Do not let your*
> *hearts tremble. Never be afraid. . . . Exert yourselves in the great*
> *battle of God! For this day is the predetermined time of battle—*
> *of the Eternal against all the nations—a judgment upon all flesh.*
> *The God of Israel raises a hand—with wondrous strength—*
> *against all the spirits of iniquity. The heroes of the "gods"*
> *array themselves to fight, but the troupe of holy ones gird*
> *themselves. . . .*
> —WAR SCROLL, col. 15:12–18

The passage can be read in two ways, as a statement of war (the "lesser jihad") or as a statement of internal, spiritual struggle (the "greater jihad"). One can imagine the "host of Satan" as describing forces within oneself, one's baser instincts, which each person must harness if one's labor is to be productive and meaningful. Read abstractly, the "warrior gods" reside in each of us, and we defeat them by our exertion, our labor.

The Sons of Light in their day were firm in the confidence that they labored not by their own might but by the power of an eternal force residing in them. Their labor, their battle, was not their own:

> *For the God of Israel, along with the Angel of Truth, will aid*
> *all the Sons of Light. Indeed, the Eternal created the spirits of*

light and the spirits of darkness, establishing every act upon their ways and every labor upon their paths.

—MANUAL OF DISCIPLINE, col. 3:24–26

Labor of Love

What do the Sons of Light teach us about labor? We learn that work is not something to do simply in order to make money, meet obligations, and pay taxes. Work is not something from which to escape during "free time" to mind-numbing "recreational activities" before we return to the grindstone all over again. Work must have meaning in and of itself. It must have value and design as well as being relevant to contemporary human society. In some way, work must make the world a better place; in some way it must make a difference. Even the most tedious, meticulous, monotonous labor can be a labor of love if it is approached from the mind-set that it is being done for a greater, metaphysical purpose—that the individual will be better for it, that humanity and the whole world will likewise be enhanced because that work has been done.

5 Time:

Cease to Be Whirled Around

As if you could kill time without *injuring eternity.*

> —Henry David Thoreau

We must use time as a tool, not as *a couch.*

> —John F. Kennedy

It haunts me, the passage of time. *I think time is a merciless thing. I think life is a process of burning oneself out and time is the fire that burns you. But I think the spirit of man is a good adversary.*

> —Tennessee Williams

❖❖❖❖❖❖❖❖❖❖❖

THESE THREE quotations illustrate three responses to one of humanity's most dogged adversaries—time. They represent the awe of time, the use of time, and the dread of time. The speakers are fairly contemporary, yet these thoughts resonate with ancient concerns addressed by the mysterious library known as the Dead Sea Scrolls.

Imagine yourself on the shores of Lake Asphaltis. Six days of labor glide by purposefully. The time you spend at work is never lost or wasted, but is "deposited" into a reservoir of meaning, a well of personal faith. Your labor is long, sometimes tedious, but never mind numbing. There isn't some distant "goal" toward which you labor, day in and day out. Rather, the time you spend in labor is its own reward. It is not a means to some other end, but an end in itself. Nevertheless, work must be subject to time, lest the value of time be forgotten.

So it is, that one day in seven you cease your labors. You rest. You reenergize your soul and with it your very existence. This day, which is also a principle, is called *Shabbat*—the Sabbath. It is a concept completely unknown in the larger, "pagan" world, from Greece to Rome in the west, to Babylonia in the east. No other people seem to understand this recurring cycle of complete rest. It seems to them such a waste, so slothful, so unproductive. Surely it is the mark of an indolent people. But for the Sons of Light, Sabbath is as consequential as life itself. For time is never to be subservient to labor; labor is subservient to time.

Anticipation

There is a definite sense of anticipation coursing through each week's labor as the hallowed day approaches. Sunrise follows sunset in a continuing cycle, through the sequence of the seven-day week. The oppressive heat of the daylight hours is replaced by the crisp cool of night. Extremes of temperature are the norm. Twilight is minimal, as the blazing sun hides itself behind the cliffs to the west, then disappears, plunging the terrain into darkness and desert chill. Day fades into day ... Day Four, Day Five, Day Six. The sixth day—what later Europeans would call

"Friday"—is almost intoxicating with its frenzy of preparation for the seventh. Time is on your mind. Time is of the essence. There is little time to be had on Day Six, and none is wasted, all in the attempt to make Day Seven hallowed, effortless.

Foods must be prepared in advance. Clay ovens are lit to bake *Shabbat* bread and to cook any number of dishes for the "queen of days," which awaits just beyond the sunset. Scribes must finish work on their parchments and store them away. Ink and quills are to be put out of sight and out of mind. All must take their turn entering the waters of purification at the *mikveh* to attain the personal measure of sanctity required to meet the "Sabbath Bride."

At last the sixth sunset approaches, ushering in the seventh day. The Secret Scrolls have declared:

> *No one will be allowed to do any work on the sixth day, from the time that the sun's great orb is the measure of its own diameter from the gate.... On the Sabbath day a person will only be allowed to eat foods that have already been prepared in advance.*

—DAMASCUS RULE, col. 10:14–16, 22

All labor ceases. The great meal, cooked hours earlier, is now consumed with joy, festivity, and celebration. Everything is symbolic of the greater meaning of this day as time comes into sharp focus, then seems to stop in its tracks. The *Shabbat* is like an island of sublime peace and tranquillity separated from a "mainland" of worldly concerns. It is a statement of eternal "being," the existential "now" of living.

All such "peculiarities" are recorded in detail by the ancient historian:

Moreover, they are stricter than any other of the Jews in rest-
ing from their labors on the seventh day; for they not only get
their food ready the day before, that they may not be obliged
to kindle a fire on that day, but they will not remove any ves-
sel out of its place.

—Josephus, WARS, II, VIII, 9

Sabbath Healing

No matter how much one is buffeted and bruised from a
week's worth of trafficking in the physical world, the Sabbath
is a time to be rejuvenated, bandaged, and healed. For twenty-
four resplendent hours, wrongs are forgiven, failings over-
looked, and the entire community comes together for mutual
support and uplifting. While all Israelites of antiquity kept the
Sabbath to one degree or another, the Sons of Light were the
most dedicated Sabbath-keepers of all. The Sabbath was
viewed by the community as a fortress, a defensive bastion
against the outside world. The Dead Sea Psalms declare:

I thank You, O Eternal, for You are like a mighty wall round
about me. You defend me against all those who bring destruc-
tion. You shelter me from raging calamity.

—PSALMS SCROLL, col. 11:37–40

You have placed my feet upon solid rock. You guide me in the
eternal Way and in the pathways that You have chosen.

—PSALMS SCROLL, col. 12:3–4

The "eternal way," as the Sons of Light understood it, very
much included the Sabbath. Let the nations scoff; let them scorn
the desert sect for their "idleness." To be a Son of Light was to
invite the jealous wrath of the whole world. But the Essenes
were not to be swayed, for the Secret Scrolls admonished:

The wicked among the nations have harried me—venting the
rage of their misfortunes against me. All day long they
depress my very soul.
—PSALMS SCROLL, col. 13:17

Without the island of the Sabbath one is defenseless against the provocations of the outside world. One is equally defenseless against the ceaseless stress of daily life and the ensuing pressure of participating in the frenetic activity of polite and not-so-polite society:

It is as though I am buffeted by a whirlwind. There is no calm,
no quiet place to restore my soul. There is no path by which to
find my way on the face of the vast waters. For the great depths
reverberate in tandem with my own moaning. My soul has
approached the very gates of death. Yet, I will be like one who
enters a fortress city—like one who finds asylum behind a high
wall—until my salvation comes.
—PSALMS SCROLL, col. 14:23–25

No wonder Israel's sages of old taught that humanity is not made for the Sabbath, but the Sabbath for humanity. It was to be a gift of joy, a balm of healing, without which the stress of living consumes us. The concept of Sabbath ultimately rises above any one particular religious orientation. Regardless of one's spiritual frame of reference, the weekly restoration of one's soul is a basic human need, on a par with food, air, water, and sleep.

A New and Better Way

Twentieth-century philosopher Abraham Joshua Heschel made some very profound observations about the celebration of time as well as time's relation to space. He wrote:

*We are all infatuated with the splendor of space, with the
grandeur of things of space.... The result of our "thinginess"
is our blindness to all reality that fails to identify itself as a
thing.*[15]

—Abraham Joshua Heschel

For generations the Sons of Light were captivated by the
splendor of Jerusalem, the grandeur of the holy Temple, and
the material pleasures afforded by a city that wallowed in its
own extravagance. The Secret Scrolls describe the transformation that took place when the members of the sect realized the
nature of their blindness, their empty materialism—the way
they were before the Teacher of Righteousness revealed a new
and better path:

*They discerned their own iniquity. They understood that they
were full of guilt. They were like blind people. For twenty years
they were like people who grope for a way in the darkness.*
—Damascus Rule, col. 1:8–10

Today we are groping in the same way, consumed by a
ceaseless quest. People may not vocalize their angst, talking instead about the things they have or would like to have. But the
dread persists, consuming the soul. Why this inherent unease,
this lack of satisfaction with materiality?

*We know what to do with space but do not know what to do
about time, except to make it subservient to space. As a result
we suffer from a deeply rooted dread of time and stand
aghast when compelled to look into its face. Time to us is sar-
casm, a slick treacherous monster with a jaw like a furnace
incinerating every moment of our lives. Shrinking, therefore,
from facing time, we escape for shelter to things of space. The*

intentions we are unable to carry out we deposit in space;
possessions become the symbols of our repressions, jubilees of
frustrations. But things of space are not fireproof; they only
add fuel to the flames.[16]
—Abraham Joshua Heschel

The Secret Scrolls had much to say to the Sons of Light
about things and "thinginess." As we saw in chapter 1, those
who pursued materiality, blind to the true reality of time, were
known as "seekers after smooth things." The *Nahum Com-*
mentary, after quoting a fearful passage from the ancient
prophet ("The prowler is not wanting. . . . There is no end to
the corpses."), declares:

The interpretation of this passage concerns the rulership of those
who seek smooth things. The sword of the gentile nations will
never be lacking from the midst of their assembly—nor will they
be lacking enslavement, pillage, or conflagration. . . . They will
even topple over their own fleshy bodies, due to the guilty coun-
sel they have disseminated.

—NAHUM COMMENTARY, frags. 3–4, col. 2:4–6

By joining the company of the Many, by casting their lot
with the community of the redeemed, the ancient Essenes
sought to liberate themselves from the quest for things and
"thinginess." They were given a revelation of time, of the
metaphysical beauty of the rest day and the sacred festivals:

As for those who firmly grasp the commandments of the
Eternal—the remnant among the people—a Covenant has been
established with Israel, forever. Hidden things—by which all
Israel have gone astray—have been revealed to them.

—DAMASCUS RULE, col. 3:12–14

What exactly were those "hidden things" that caused the Sons of Light to depart from the company of the material-minded? The text continues:

> *The holy Sabbaths and the feasts of glory, testimonies of justice and paths of truth, the desires of the divine will—all these shall a person keep, and live by them.*
> —DAMASCUS RULE, col. 3:14–16

Those who understand time and how to pause regularly before the wonder of life are the ones who shall live and prosper on the good earth. They have dug for themselves a well of life. But those who confuse time with things, who prefer the illusion of materiality to the reality of time, shall perish. The scrolls explain how the Sons of Light were rescued from the path of materiality and led toward a new destiny:

> *They dug out a well of abundant water, but whoever turns aside from it will not live. Nevertheless, they floundered in human iniquity and in paths of uncleanness. They exclaimed, "This path is ours!" However, the Eternal, in accord with the wonderful secrets, acquitted them from all their iniquity and forgave them for their evil deeds. The Eternal constructed for them a steadfast house in Israel, the likes of which has never arisen, from hoary antiquity until now.*
> —DAMASCUS RULE, col. 3:16–20

What is the "house in Israel" built on behalf of the Sons of Light? It is not a physical abode but a sanctuary of time, meted out in holy days—a divine cadence, where past and present seem to stand still before the immanence of holiness. The scroll continues, declaring that for those who recognize this greater reality, time itself shall eventually disappear in eternity:

Surely, those who firmly grasp it will live forever. All of
Adam's primordial glory will belong to them.
—DAMASCUS RULE, col. 3:20

Being versus Doing

Like the earliest Christians—fellow Judeans who have
freely borrowed some of the Essenes' deepest principles—the
Sons of Light understood intimately that sufficient time must
be devoted to the process of "being" rather than "doing." This
is perhaps life's greatest lesson of all. It is not only true that
mindless materialism leaves us empty; materiality alone means
that we do not know the value of time. We are actually afraid
of time, as well as meaning and value; and this is why we turn
to materialism. We fill our lives with toys because we are afraid
to face head-on the meaning of our lives and the contributions
we may or may not be making. Such observations are couched
in the wisdom of Israel's ancient sages. No one understood that
wisdom and put it into practice better than the covenantal
community on the shores of the Dead Sea. This is why the community rule books were so careful to prohibit on the Sabbath
day anything remotely connected with the material world, even
talking about such things:

> *No one is to make any decisions with regard to material*
> *things or financial gain. No one is to mention anything about*
> *work, or even about labor to be done on the following day.*
> —DAMASCUS RULE, col. 10:17–19

Not only did the Sons of Light respect the principle of
Sabbath above all their compatriots in ancient Judea; they also
recognized that things must be subservient to time, not the
other way around. That explains why they prohibited every-

thing that might distract them from the metaphysical purpose of the seventh day. The prohibitions for members of the community are numerous and, at first glance, seem rigid and restrictive:

- *No one is to walk out to the field, beyond the settlement—in order to fulfill his own desires—on the Sabbath day.*
- *No one is to walk a distance of more than a thousand cubits outside of the settlement.*
- *No one is to eat or drink anything outside of the settlement.*
- *No one is to fill a vessel with water.*
- *No one is to send a stranger to do business in his stead on the Sabbath day.*
- *No one is to put on dirty clothes ... unless they have already been cleaned with water or anointed with incense.*
- *No one is to lift up his hand in violence, in order to strike someone with his fist.*
- *No one is to take anything out of his house, or bring anything from the outside into his house.*
- *No one is to lift up so much as a stone or a piece of dust inside his home.*
- *No one is to desecrate the Sabbath for the sake of material things or financial gain.*
  —DAMASCUS RULE, col. 10–11

In spite of their stringency, however, these ordinances were hardly an exercise in legalism. They were a means of insuring that this day would be different from all others. They demanded that people should stop in their tracks for twenty-four hours and take stock of their lives. They made sure that materiality would not blind their adherents to the nonmaterial universe—a universe every bit as real as the one that can be seen and measured. The Sons of Light were compelled to deal with time, to look full in its face, as they welcomed the sanctity of this recurring day of rest. Rather than looking to find shelter in things, they were to look to the Sabbath itself as an island shelter. All possessions, all sustenance, all property, all assets became servants of this island in time.

The Sons of Light also realized something that moderns well understand—that if you simply tell people to relax and take it easy, they probably won't. The delirious pace of work will in all likelihood be replaced by the equally delirious activity of what goes under the name "recreation" but which is just as draining and stressful, if not more so, than the grind of labor. The Sabbath principle, more than a mere religious construct, is fundamental to individual growth and development. This is why the concept of Sabbath, unheard of until the ancestors of the Essenes, the ancient Israelites, introduced it, has nonetheless become almost universal (at least in theory) in the modern world. In Christianity the Sabbath is Sunday, in Judaism it is Saturday, in Islam it is Friday, and many other faiths have their own versions of the day of rest. But to grasp it fully, one must realize that its purpose is really not "recreation" at all, but "re-creation."

The concept is simple. In tradition it took God six days to create the universe, but on the seventh God refrained from creative activity. Likewise, humans are to refrain, not from "work" per se but from creating things externally. That is why the Sons of Light have decreed, along with the rest of the Israelite community, that one must not build, write, cook, plant, reap, or mend on the seventh day. This is because people are to focus on "re-creating" themselves. Instead of creating things external to their lives, people are to dwell on internal things, the "intangibles."

Times and Seasons

"To everything there is a season," wrote the author of the book of Ecclesiastes, "and a time to every purpose under heaven." The Sons of Light, like their Israelite counterparts, believed that specific times during the year were to be acknowledged by "holy days," set apart for a divine purpose. In addition to the Sabbath, these additional times and seasons were to serve to focus the mind, sharpen the senses, and ultimately enrich one's life. One season turns into the next, one time of sacred dedication turns to another. There is a metaphysical rhyme and reason to existence, and stopping to observe certain hallowed times makes us mindful of it:

> *The Eternal does the first things in their predetermined times*
> *and also does the last things in their designated seasons.*
> —SONG OF SABBATH SACRIFICES, Masada Fragment (4Q402) 4, 13–14

By the time the first millennium B.C.E. turned to the first millennium C.E., the Sons of Light had created their own solar calendar, distinct from the Jewish lunar calendar, and had based it on a 364-day year. The observance of special holidays served to keep their calendar intact, which in turn preserved their way of life. The covenantal community had reserved special days to commemorate various Israelite festivals, as required by the biblical text. The ultimate Sabbath was the Day of Atonement (Yom Kippur), devoted to the mortification of the flesh, which included a total fast of food and drink. On this day, which might well be conceived of as "the great equalizer," the rich and the poor, the weak and the mighty were leveled in the experience of humble repentance.

Only in the contemporary world is the full, healing power of forgiveness coming to be understood by the medical community in all its radical implications. There is no carcinogen like inward bitterness and no antioxidant like rapprochement and reconciliation between adversaries. But one must "come clean" before the Eternal and one's fellows, hiding nothing and becoming transparent. The Secret Scrolls preserve a special prayer, reserved for the holiest of all days:

A PRAYER FOR THE DAY OF ATONEMENT

Please favor us, O Eternal . . . at the time we make our peace with You. . . .

For You make us rejoice in the time of our anguish. You have gathered our scattered ones, for the time when Your loving-kindness will be showered upon Your congregation, like a stream of water upon the earth. . . .

Surely, You know all the hidden things; and you also know the revealed things. . . .

—1Q34BIS, frag. 2:1–6

The community also observed the other biblical feasts. There was Passover, which commemorates Israel's release from slavery in Egypt. There was the Feast of Weeks (*Shavuot,* also called "Pentecost" in Greek), an early wheat harvest festival that came to represent the giving of the Law to Moses on Mount Sinai. There was also the Feast of Booths (*Sukkot*), commemorating the forty-year wilderness wandering of the people of Israel, prior to entering the Land of Promise. Very much a feast of the desert, the Feast of Booths required that people should physically leave their dwellings for seven full days and sleep in rude huts with branches for roofs. It was designed once again to teach the value of time—that our earthy sojourn is temporary and that the best way to get in touch with the Eternal and with ourselves is to go back to the "desert experiences" of life. Get out of your house, your sumptuous surroundings. Simplify! See yourself as a pilgrim and a stranger on the earth.

Additionally, there was the Feast of Firstfruits, wherein the first part of the year's harvest was presented to God. Regarding this feast the following Dead Sea Scroll fragment speaks:

A PRAYER FOR THE FEAST OF FIRSTFRUITS

Please favor us, O Eternal, on this Feast of Firstfruits. Please accept the pleasant, freewill offerings, which You commanded us to render unto You. For we have presented before You the firstfruits of Your works....
—4Q509III, frag. 132:5–7

The central idea here is that everything in nature is seen as the work of the Eternal, and that one must stop in time at the beginning of the harvest to acknowledge the divine sovereignty. This was done by presenting the first part of the harvest as an offering, so that all labor done thereafter would honor God's supremacy in creation. The very notion that this offering is "first" suggests that acknowledging the Creator must, chronologically, come before anything else.

In addition to feast days prescribed by the biblical text, the Sons of Light have added their own special festivals. There was an annual festival for the Renewal of the Covenant, at which time Essenes from all over Judea would converge for days of feasting, designed to reaffirm the uniqueness of their community and cement their bond of mutual trust and fellowship. There were additional holidays—delineated in the longest of the Secret Scrolls, the famous *Temple Scroll*—namely, the Feast of New Oil, the Feast of New Wine, and the Feast of Wood:

... the festival days of the Firstfruits: of the grain harvest; of the new wine, and of the oil—and the days for offering wood. A tithe is to be eaten on these days. Nothing of it is to be left over from one year to the next. This is the manner in which everyone is to eat it.

—TEMPLE SCROLL, col. 43:3–5

The first section of this part of the scroll has suffered damage. Little is known about these feasts beyond what remains. How were these feasts celebrated? What particular rituals must have accompanied the consumption of a tenth (a tithe) of the grain harvest, a tenth of the new wine, and a tenth of the oil? In what manner was wood to be burned as an offering? Such details are consigned to the realm of speculation. All that can be discerned from the ancient text itself is the date of the festivals. The Firstfruits of the grain harvest corresponds with the Jewish Feast of Weeks (*Shavuot*) and was to be held on the fifteenth day of the third month. The New Wine Festival was to occur on the third day of the fifth month. The New Oil Festival was to be held on the twenty-second day of the sixth month. The Wood Festival was consigned to some period between the twenty-third and the thirtieth day of the sixth month. The months themselves follow the sect's solar calendar, in which the spring festival of Passover falls on the fourteenth day of the first month. Nothing else about these feasts is certain, but one thing seems clear: Life, in all its vicissitudes, is an endless cycle of celebration, and those who came to the desert were constantly reminded of its primal, fundamental festivity.

The Eclipse of Time

One of the most serious illusions possessed by Homo sapiens is that time is, in some mysterious way, absolute. It is seen as a fixed, changeless entity by which all things grow and all things eventually decay. It is perceived as an immutable constant in an impersonal universe, where little is certain and where most hallowed wisdom is challenged, undermined, and negated.

The Secret Scrolls take a different view. Far from immutable, the Sons of Light understood time to be a human construct, destined to disappear. It is a feeble human attempt to explain what appears to us as change but is in reality the mere unfolding of all things foreordained, held within the mind of the Eternal, for whom the beginning and the end are one and the same.

Astrophysicists refer to time as a function of the second law of thermodynamics, also called entropy. It is the principle that explains how all matter in the universe proceeds from a state of order to a state of disorder. What human beings measure as time is only the outworking of the entropy principle, the full measure of which is subsumed in the mind of "God," however God may be conceived. Einstein said as much. Space and time are indeed linked, physically as well as philosophically, though not as constants. They are a continuum, in a constant dance with each other. This is why, when we fail to appreciate time, we flee to things of space. This is why, on a metaphysical level, "The intentions we are unable to carry out we deposit in space."

We imagine, naively, that there is always another day, more time out ahead. We conveniently forget that the only thing that counts is the eternal "now." The end and the beginning are both the same in the eyes of the Eternal. Time itself is eclipsed. Deity, unaffected by the laws of thermodynamics, is quite beyond time, "seeing," as it were, all events in history as occurring simultaneously. The Secret Scrolls have much to say about what subsequent theologians would call "predestination," the idea that the fate of individuals is determined by God before birth. They nonetheless indicate that we are not helpless before the divine will, forcing us to make one choice or another.

Rather than fretting about this or that bend in the road, whether we made the right decision here, the wrong decision there, we are told that such preoccupations are utterly irrelevant. The Eternal sees everything in the present tense, from the moment of conception to the moment of death. The pressure to make "right" decisions is lessened, if not removed; for in the realm beyond time, our decisions are known before we make them. We are to rest, therefore, in each moment, savoring the present, knowing that nothing beyond each instant in which we draw our breath matters in the grand scheme of things. Time is eclipsed. One of the community rule books decrees:

> *The Eternal knew all of their works, before they were even begun—from the beginning of time. . . . The Eternal foreknew the precise years in which they would take shape, as well as the exact duration of their existence. The Eternal foreknew all that would happen through all ages—until all that was destined occurs in their appointed times, throughout all eternity. In all of those times, the Eternal raised up individuals called by name—a righteous remnant—which will be left in the land. In the end, the whole world will be filled with their offspring.*
> —DAMASCUS RULE, col. 2:7–12

What freedom, what internal equanimity is yielded through this confident assertion that we are connected with the One beyond, that our lives are not the result of blind chance. We are to know that divine order leads us, follows us, surrounds us. Time becomes our servant, not our enemy. The words of King David of old are recalled:

I trust in you, O Eternal.
I say, "You are my God."
My times are in your hands.
—PSALM 31:14–15

I Vill a Little T'ink

There is a natural human tendency to be impulsive, to jump to conclusions, often with devastating consequences. A fast-food culture demands quick solutions, slick answers, programmed responses. Abstractions are not tolerated. All is reduced to the lowest common denominator. There is little stomach for mystery in a culture that wants what it wants and wants it now. People can feel threatened by abstractions, as if their cozy little worlds will cave in if they allow their accepted belief systems to be challenged. This is not the way of the Sons of Light. They had been taught to recognize the mystery that pervades the universe, to appreciate that every breath taken is part of the divine secret called life. Better still, they were admonished to take the time to explore the mystery, not from the shallow vessel of brittle "theology," but by taking deep drafts of that which is normally beyond human grasp. Roman philosopher-emperor Marcus Aurelius wrote:

> *Do the things external which fall upon thee distract thee?*
> *Give thyself time to learn something new and good, and cease*
> *to be whirled around.*
> —Marcus Aurelius, MEDITATIONS, Book II, 7

Albert Einstein, when immersed in work on some difficult problem, would often demur, recognizing the importance of taking time to consider a matter, to ponder it fully. His somewhat eccentric behavior was recorded by a colleague:

> *When it became clear that [we could not solve a problem],*
> *Einstein would stand up quietly and say, in his quaint*
> *English, "I vill a little t'ink." So saying, he would pace up*
> *and down or walk around in circles, all the time twirling a*
> *lock of his long, graying hair around his finger.*[17]

We should all learn to pace, to take the time, and even to walk around in circles. It is one of the most liberating things a person can do. Einstein knew instinctively that time must be subservient to the process of thinking, that the crush of external pressures obliterates creative thought, that one must momentarily step out of one's time-governed thoughts in order to master them. "I vill a little t'ink." It was all he needed to say.

In fact, true, creative thought is not only beyond the realm of time, it is beyond the artificial boundaries imposed by words. Einstein also commented:

> *Words or language, as they are written or spoken, do not*
> *seem to play any role in my mechanism of thought.*[18]

Likewise, we should all give ourselves time to experience true thought, to travel the ancient meditative path that lies beyond time, uncluttered by syllables. All else is peripheral. Discover the "Word" beyond words, everlasting and unmolested by time:

> *You have whispered new things into an ear of dust. You have*
> *carved eternal things into a heart of stone.*
> —PSALMS SCROLL, col. 21:12–13

Method Out of Madness

The archaeology reveals the truth about the Sons of Light. They hardly lived pastoral, countrified lives, uncorrupted by complexity; instead they were technologically quite advanced for their day and age. Why did the pressures of running a large and intricate desert society not encroach upon the hallowed time they had sought to preserve by coming to this place? The answer is in their method—the consistent pattern by which they ran their affairs. The Secret Scrolls give us a hint of their daily routine, circumscribed by meditative prayer, which ordered their lives, making time all the more their servant. They were deeply aware of the passage of the hours, the arc of the sun in the sky, and they ordered their agenda by its position:

> *Falling down before You, I will appeal to You continually . . . when the light first dawns—coming to rule the day—and throughout the course of the day. It is all in harmony with the precepts, determined by the Great Light of Heaven. When the light sinks again, in the evening hours, the darkness begins to rule in its stead. At that time comes the hour for the rule of the night. Finally, another morning dawns. The darkness always goes back to its retreat, before the sun rises again. At the very beginning of each period of time—at the dawning of every age— and throughout the progress of each season—by virtue of the precepts and the signs, assigned for their jurisdiction—all is by direct order from the mouth of the Eternal and by the testimony of all that is. All of this will come to pass—nothing more or less. Aside from this there is nothing. Neither will there be anything else forever.*
>
> —PSALMS SCROLL, col. 20:4–10

The awe of the "great light of heaven" was very much a part of the intrinsic order of the Essenes' life, for their daily routine was governed by the precise position of the sun in the sky. This helps explain the fact that they created a solar calendar, unique in Jewish tradition, wherein a lunar calendar is the norm. In recent years what has been identified as a sundial was discovered at the site of Qumran. The Sons of Light used it to divide a day into a series of twelve "hours" of equal length. Of course, each "hour" would be longer in the summer and shorter in the winter. The day was divided into three watches, sunrise, noon (or the "fifth hour"), and sunset. It was immensely important to find the "fifth hour," the exact time when the covenantal meal was consumed at the settlement, the time when the members of community aligned themselves with heaven. They believed that this true alignment with heaven would one day culminate in a war with the Sons of Darkness—an eschatological end to time itself.[19] But in the meantime they delighted in the divine pattern of the days, seizing each moment.

Patience Please

The writers of the Secret Scrolls were patient, long-suffering, and steadfast; they knew that when time is subservient to people, and not vice versa, there is plenty of it. Settlements were not constructed in a day, nor were the scrolls copied in haste. Caves were dug into limestone cliffs by one blow of hammer and chisel after another, methodically, over long days, weeks, and the passing of seasons. The copying of a single text could take months, and the copying of the entire canon of biblical texts (still being formulated in those days) could take years. The acquisition of the scribal arts, a labor in which the Sons of Light prided themselves, not only required patience; it developed patience in all who desired to learn it.

The Sons of Light, who carried the charge of bringing perfection to Israel, greatly needed patience, for they shouldered a mighty burden. The Messiah, it is said, shall come in the manner predicted by the prophet Zechariah: "humble and riding on an ass" (Zechariah 9:9). The members of this covenantal community were like a patient beast of burden, the ass upon which the Anointed One rides, trudging slowly onward down the long and winding road, uncomplaining in their allotted task:

> *May each person order every step—in order to walk in perfection and simplicity—in all the ways of the Eternal. This is what is commanded with regard to the appointed times and the holy convocations. Do not stray from the path, either to the right or to the left!*
> —MANUAL OF DISCIPLINE, col. 3:9–10

Such is the essence of patience. Patience involves time and its mastery. When we lose our dread of time, we are able to set our hands with steadiness of purpose to those tasks that seem to take so much of it. Time's great lesson is that the joy is in the journey.

6 Learning:
Sanctuaries of Wonder

A LITTLE LEARNING IS A DANGEROUS
thing;
*Drink deep, or taste not the Pierian
spring;*
*There shallow draughts intoxicate the
brain,*
And drinking largely sobers us again.

—Alexander Pope

TAKE YOURSELF back to the desert community of the great rift valley of the Jordan River. Imagine your place among the Many, the society of the Sons of Light. You have come here not to pursue selfish ambition but to find a better way of living, to become a better human being. Finding this way, however, involves discipline and a level of commitment and sacrifice, both physical and mental. The Secret Scrolls explain what this way entails, as you seek to become one of the Many:

> *When these individuals join the Community in Israel, becoming members—as all of the rules have dictated—they will be sepa-*

*rated from the dwelling place of the unrighteous. They will go
into the desert, to prepare in that place the Way of the Eternal.
This is what is written by the prophet (Isaiah 40:3): "Prepare in
the wilderness the way of the Lord, make straight in the desert a
path for our God." This "way" involves the diligent study of the
Law. This is what Moses himself commanded—to perform all
things that have been laid open from age to age, and to do what
the Prophets have revealed, according to the Holy Spirit.*

—MANUAL OF DISCIPLINE, col. 8:12–15

Study versus Good Deeds

A great question arose in ancient Israel: Which is more important, study or action, the careful scrutiny of the sacred texts or the performance of good deeds? Ancient Israelites were clearly divided into schools of thought on this important subject. The great rabbi Hillel and his disciples insisted that study is the most important thing to pursue, for it leads to the performance of good deeds:

*The more Torah, the more life.... If someone has acquired a
good name, he has done it for his own sake. But if someone has
acquired the teaching of the Torah, he has acquired eternal life.*

—MISHNAH AVOT 2:7

Others, including the towering sage Shimon ben Gamliel, declared that doing good deeds is supremely important in life:

It is not learning but doing that is the most important thing.

—MISHNAH AVOT 1:17

Likewise the ancient Hasidic sage Hanina ben Dosa said:

Wisdom is not on a par with good deeds.

—MISHNAH AVOT 3:12

Jesus of Nazareth seems to have taken the same side, for he declared:

Let your light so shine before men, that they may see your good deeds and give glory to your Father who is in heaven.
—MATTHEW 5:16

Who won the debate? The performance of good deeds became one of the pillars of the Jewish faith, but without question the argument was won by Hillel, whose name is hallowed in Jewish lore and whom Jews have forever admired for stressing the importance of learning. The Secret Scrolls, while they didn't settle the argument then and there, certainly redounded to Hillel's favor, for their message is that study is paramount. An ignorant, unlearned person may believe that he or she is performing good deeds when in fact this is not the case. How can one know what deeds are truly good if one has not been devoted to the study of ethics as embodied in the sacred texts? Study is integral to the whole of life, for it remakes every individual from the inside out. It establishes the very steps that determine a person's way.

The Sons of Light took the prophet Isaiah literally. They came to the wilderness to face the oppressive heat, the blinding sun, the chalky dust beneath their feet, and the sulfurous lake of salt. They took their oaths, repeatedly purified themselves with water, and went through a lengthy period of initiation. But their commitment did not end there. The path they sought was more than a road through the desert sands. The road they embarked on was not physical; it was ethical. The path was nothing more or less than the study of the Law—the Torah—revealed to Moses on Mount Sinai. It involved, at the heart of it all, the training of the mind.

Modern people should recognize that study is the least tangible, yet the most important of all disciplines, because it grounds your soul in a transcendental reality, in a truth beyond oneself. It enables you to devote your life not to pleasure for pleasure's sake, but to truth for truth's sake. Only through study can you avoid being "whirled around" by confusing currents of ideology. Only through study can you find out who you are, where you have come from, the heritage that belongs to you, and the destiny to which you are headed.

Wrestling

The Sons of Light were to "gird up the loins of their mind." The study they undertook, as the Overseer of the community had taught, was a battle of sorts. It involved a great cosmic conflict in which the members of the covenant were to take part. They were to play an active role in a metaphysical battle, and they did so by nothing more or less profound than the study they engaged in. In study they became part of a greater reality, an eternal purpose. They not only improved themselves, but they also released energy into the cosmos, which in turn would affect the higher realms, over and above all.

They were asked to submit their minds to discipline. Yet this was no blind submission, for this kind of study involved questioning, reflecting on, and wrestling with every word of the sacred text. They were called to faith, but this kind of faith did not demand the abrogation of their minds but the sharpening of their intellect. The doctrines they held were worked out through long study sessions in which the Many deliberated together.

The Sons of Light were not all great sages, but every one of them could read and write They were all devoted students, thinking for themselves, and this fact was one of their greatest strengths. Each of them was trained in finding the desert path, and they understood that people who are so educated can never be enslaved. Their proclaimed foes to the west, the Romans, had coined a saying, "He who buys an Israelite slave has bought himself a master." For one who trains the mind is a very poor subject for imposed tyranny. There is freedom in study, liberty in the acquisition of wisdom.

This is why the Sons of Light were taught to wrestle with the holy texts, even as they laboriously learned to copy them. Biblical parchments to this day teach the reader an awesome lesson. They are made of the skin of kosher animals, soaked in lime solution for many days, stretched out on wooden frames, cut to size, and sewn together. But it is the threads, holding each section of the sacred scrolls in place, which convey something deeply symbolic. They are taken not from just any part of the animal, but from the area of the thigh—the sciatic nerve, to be precise. This is to remind all who approach the text of how Jacob, the patriarch of Israel's twelve tribes, was confronted at night by an angel, who wrestled with him until the break of day. When Jacob held his own, refusing to give in and demanding a blessing, the angel changed his name to "Israel"—"Prince of God." But the angel struck Jacob in his thigh, and from that day on he walked with a limp. In a similar fashion, we can be certain that every time the Sons of Light took up the inspired text to read from it, they did not approach it passively. They engaged the text; they interacted with it; they wrestled with it. They took nothing for granted. They asked questions, about each and every word. Why is it stated like this and not some other way? Why is this word used and not some other? Thus they grappled with the inspired word, wrestling even with God who gave it. This process was not a measure of unbelief but a measure of the strongest faith, a faith that dares to ask why.

Acquiring the Precepts

Wisdom was highly prized by the Sons of Light, and in the Essene communities outside of the Dead Sea settlement, females as well as males were to partake thereof. How many other ancient cultures can boast that women were to be educated just as young men? Most women in the Greco-Roman world were treated as nothing more than chattel, and on this score the Essenes were well ahead of their time. The Secret Scrolls declare:

> *All those who come together will be properly assembled. This includes the little children and the women. At that time they will read into their ears all the ordinances of the Covenant. They will teach them all of their decrees, so that they will not commit grave mistakes.*
> —MESSIANIC RULE, col. 1:4–5

There was a mysterious volume referred to in the Secret Scrolls as the *Book of Meditation,* which has never been found. But we are told that the young were to be tutored in its wisdom. Whatever, precisely, the *Book of Meditation* was, it seems to have contained the "ordinances of the Covenant"—foundational principles that galvanized the community around its solemn pact, its "covenant," with God. For ten consecutive years children were to be "educated in their statutes."

The Sons of Light were quite ordinary. They came from a broad spectrum of society, and not necessarily the most "elite" or affluent segments of Judean society. What set them apart was their discipline and their dedication, which translated into an impressive level of literacy and an equally impressive level of general and religious knowledge.

Memory

It is said that faith is memory. The statement is as profound as it is simple. Experience had taught the Sons of Light that what one believes is shaped by what the individual, in the company of the Many, remembers about his heritage. Faith was not to be blind. It was not a matter of unbridled emotion, fervent passion, or even religious sentimentalism. Nor was faith a private matter. It wasn't subject to what one feels or imagines individually. It was a shared record of how the Eternal has dealt with each individual and with the entire community. For this reason the rules of the Many required that the reading and study of the sacred texts were to be conducted in groups of no fewer than ten: the legacy of their faith was a record to be studied in unison.

God needed no objective proof for existence beyond the fact that God's people exist. There was a sense that the Many had traveled together on a journey through the centuries, from the foot of Mount Sinai to the shore of Lake Asphaltis, from that distant mountain to this arid plain. Abraham and Sarah, Isaac and Rebecca, Jacob, Rachel and Leah, Moses and all the prophets—their experience belonged to the Many, for they had journeyed in their seed.

This is why they studied the ancient texts. This is why they copied the sacred scrolls, for they contained the collected memories of the Many and of all Israel. They cataloged the birth of a desert nation, a group of strangers and pilgrims, much like the Sons of Light. They narrated their story, from slavery in Egypt, to glorious liberation, to a generation of wilderness sojournings, to final entrance to the Land of Promise. In these writings the Many found their identity, their strength, themselves. When they were tossed about and buffeted, they returned to the sacred texts. When besieged, these writings became their refuge and stronghold. When assailed, the sacred writings became their weapons. The scrolls of the Judean desert contain a certain militancy in tone and in content. But this militancy should not be mistaken for aggression. It is simply a bold faith in the power of knowledge to deliver and to set free the body and the soul.

Even as the Sons of Light wrestled with the text, they devoted themselves not only to studying it but also to memorizing it. The holy words were something they lived with, reciting and chanting them to harmonious melodies, throughout the day and into the night. They became one with the words, and the words became a part of them. Verse by verse, passage by passage, they committed the scrolls to memory. Some among their company memorized virtually the entire sacred canon— the books of Moses, the Prophets, and the assorted writings of the biblical text. It seems like a monumental task, yet it is one to which the members of the sect gladly gave their life's energy. Others among their troupe memorized a mélange of additional books, letters, and treatises, the literary product of the great library of the Sons of Light. They included a host of writings to which moderns would assign their own titles: the *War Scroll,* the *Manual of Discipline,* the *Genesis Apocryphon,* the *Damascus Rule,* and a great many others. There was no want of material to commit to memory. But this was the chief discipline of the community; it was the "path," the way in the wilderness. As it is written:

> *Wherever ten individuals are gathered together, there will never be lacking a single individual among them. For they are to study the Law at all times, by day and by night, in shifts, one being relieved by another. The Many will share in keeping watch together.*

They will do this for a third of each night, through the course of
the year. Thus, they will read the Book and study the ordinances.
—MANUAL OF DISCIPLINE, col. 6:6–7

People of the Book, People of Judgment

The Israelites (the Sons of Light included) came to be
called "People of the Book." This means that they developed a
reverence for the inscribed word. It means that they possessed
a faith in the betterment of humanity, which was facilitated
through appropriating the wisdom of the ages. It means that
they believed in ethics, morality, and justice and that such commodities are written in the universe and are in fact attainable.
Again and again, the Secret Scrolls stress the acquisition of
knowledge:

The Eternal loves knowledge, having brought true wisdom and
knowledge before the divine presence. Indeed, discretion and
knowledge are servants of the Eternal.
—DAMASCUS RULE, col. 2:3–4

The quest for knowledge is like a physical thirst. It is like
craving water in a dry and thirsty land. When the Sons of Light
received instruction, when they sat in study sessions with their
fellows, it was like a rain shower that suddenly materializes,
turning the wadis to raging torrents and restoring life to the
land of death. Knowledge is like water, seeking a vessel into
which to be poured. Each member of the ancient community
became that vessel. The water filled them; it became them.
Without water, without knowledge, they would shrivel and die.
There was no other option, no other way. To study is to live.
Furthermore, there was the idea that when a Son of Light stud-

ied, he was actually receiving instruction from supernatural beings in the heavenly realm—the angels. One of the blessings found in the scrolls reads:

> *May the Eternal bless you with every blessing from the holy residence and from the eternal spring—that which will never dry up.*
>
> *May the Eternal honor you with every spiritual blessing, instructing you in the knowledge of the saints. May the Eternal open an unending fountain for you, never holding back water from the thirsty ones.*
>
> —BLESSINGS (1QSb), col. 1:3–6

Of course the angels were to work hand in hand with human representatives. Study was not to be chaotic and haphazard, but the orderly function of a community of faith. In another of the Secret Scrolls texts, the Eternal personally declares:

> *When I have finished establishing the Covenant and decreeing the Way in which you are to walk, I want you to appoint wise sages. They will explain all these precepts of the Law to you and to all your children.*
>
> —THE WORDS OF MOSES (1Q22), col. 2:7–9

A direct by-product of a wise and knowledgeable community is a just community. Moreover, a trained mind is, more often than not, a fine legal mind. In the case of the Sons of Light, they clearly policed their own affairs, devoting several of their documents—including the *Damascus Rule* and the *Manual of Discipline*—to legal matters and to the rules governing their society. It was through the wisdom of their judgments that their community, living in one of the harshest climates on earth, managed to survive and to flourish for two full centuries. While provisions had been made for selecting ten individuals to act as judges, it appears that in many instances the entire community sat as a deliberative body. Incredible as it sounds, in a land where tyrants ruled in Jerusalem, they created a genuine "democracy." And democracies, if they are to succeed, invariably require that the participants possess wisdom and knowledge, which can only come through learning. One of the community rule books reads:

> THIS IS THE RULE FOR THE CONGRESS OF THE MANY
>
> *Every individual will be seated by rank. The priests will be seated first—then, the elders—then, the remainder of the people will be seated, each in the order of his rank. Then, they will be examined regarding the precepts of the Law. They will be questioned about any advice or other matter, taken up by the Many. Each will make his knowledge available to the Council of the Community.*
>
> —MANUAL OF DISCIPLINE, col. 6:8–10

Additionally, the ancient historian writes:

> *But in the judgments they exercise they are most accurate and just; nor do they pass sentence by the votes of a court that is fewer than a hundred. And as to what is once determined by that number, it is unalterable. What they most of all honor, after God himself, is the name of their legislator [Moses;] whom, if any one blaspheme, he is punished capitally. They also think it a good thing to obey their elders.*
>
> —Josephus, WARS, II, VIII, 9

The Healthy Way

The lifestyle of the Sons of Light clearly represents another by-product of their study. The members of the covenantal community recognized something that moderns have thoroughly lost sight of—that the discipline of learning provides cohesion, a clear and compelling reason for being. Study was the "glue" for their whole society. It gave them purpose and became for them the driving force behind their work and their labors. Furthermore, in learning to be analytical rather than blindly submissive, they had nothing to fear from the writings they studied. Instead they were able to cull from them what was advantageous, both physically and metaphysically. The flow of knowledge was free, their minds and souls unfettered.

Some researchers are so impressed by the wide array of literature, from the many genres represented among the Secret Scrolls (psalms and hymns; apocalyptic writings and visions; a rule book that refers to raising families, the *Damascus Rule*—and another rule book that does not, the *Manual of Discipline*; mystical texts; commentaries on biblical books; blessings and benedictions), that they find it hard to believe that this is all the product of a single religious order. According to these scholars, the texts of Qumran must be the compiled writings of several different sects of ancient Judea, which simply happen to have been brought to the desert and deposited in the caves for safekeeping. But such arguments fail to take into account the considerable room for pluralism among the ideas of the Essenes. For example, how many messiahs might there be, one or two? Can people be delivered through military might, or should they trust solely in God? Is single life the best way, or should all those among the Many continue to marry and raise families? While certain ideas were doubtless shared by the whole community, the nature of study is that it tends to free the individual from the intellectual straitjacket of imposed ideology. While the "path" itself consisted of study, there were many different directions in which the path might lead.

One of those paths appears to have been searching out healthy ways to live, and the adoption of a lifestyle conducive to long life and happiness. According to the ancient historian, the pursuit of herbal remedies for all manner of ailments was a major part of their discipline. Bear in mind, there were many other writings in the ancient world (beyond the biblical scrolls), which, while not surviving to the present, were certainly familiar to the Essenes. As the Sons of Light studied these writings, their entire community must surely have gained a deep understanding of how to treat common maladies naturally, using substances common to their desert environment. The historian writes:

> *They also take great pains in studying the writings of the ancients, and choose out of them what is most for the advantage of their soul and body; and they inquire after such roots and medicinal stones as may cure their distempers.*
> —Josephus, WARS, II, VIII, 6

What "roots and medicinal stones" did they find in the wilderness of Judea that were capable of making them whole in body, just as their religious disciplines made them whole in spirit? Sadly, our knowledge of such things is minimal, and we moderns can only wonder what the ancients knew and that we have forgotten.

The Forgotten Discipline

The great Dead Sea rule book boasts:

> *I will surround my knowledge with judicious counsel. I will enclose it with discreet wisdom, as with a fence.*
> —MANUAL OF DISCIPLINE, col. 10:24–25

We know instinctively that success in anything requires training and discipline. In modern Western, technological society, we find ourselves stressing education more than ever, yet ironically flinching from the most basic disciplines of education—study and memory. Scholastic requirements of memorization are deemed stale and outdated, a "boxing in" of young minds, and the emphasis is on freshness and innovation. Unfortunately, in casting aside the hard work of memory, we are producing generations of youth who are profoundly adrift in the world, unable to relate to any common heritage that might bind them together as a people and a nation. For example, a recent study at a major East Coast university revealed that the majority of college freshmen were unable to identify in which century the Civil War was fought! On a midwestern campus, a similar group of college students was unable to identify on a map the difference between Israel and Spain! Clearly, it is no exaggeration to say that we have forgotten how to study.

Without question the great religious cultures of the Western world—Judaism, Christianity, and Islam—possess a wealth of material to study and a vast heritage from which to learn. In the footsteps of the society of the Sons of Light have come a multitude of rabbis, Christian clerics, and Muslim scholars, who filled libraries with the wisdom of their accumulated traditions. Yet many contemporary seekers, regardless of their cultural heritage, reduce religious experience to raw emotion, seeking an ecstatic "high" without realizing that emotions drift and plummet just as they build and rise. Inevitably, disillusionment comes when expectations are not fully met. In the final analysis, deeply felt faith must be grounded in knowledge.

There was no greater admonition among the Sons of Light than to encourage all among the community to develop the discipline of study:

At this time, my people, listen to me! Give ear to me, you simple ones! Make yourselves wise by means of the Eternal's power. Resolve to remember the wonders performed in the land of Egypt, and the great signs done in the land of Ham. Tremble with the fear of the Eternal! Perform the divine will. Open your minds to lovingkindness and goodness. Earnestly seek for yourselves the Way to life!

—EXHORTATION TO SEEK WISDOM, frags. 1–2, col. 1:13–15; col. 2:1–2

The Greatest of Sages

The great emphasis placed by the Sons of Light on the merit of study is exemplified in the life of one of the greatest ancient sages of all. His name was Akiva. According to the traditional account, he was born a son of impoverished parents and labored as a shepherd until adulthood. Akiva's saintly wife, knowing that her husband had a special "gift" for inquiry, sold her hair so that her husband could afford to study. The humble shepherd studied until he became a towering sage. His wisdom and knowledge were widely recognized, and he took up the mantle of spiritual leadership among his people. It was said that for forty years Akiva was an ignorant man; for forty years he studied; and for forty years he ruled Israel. It is one more testimony to the power of study.

Nor is it an accident that the term by which synagogues came to be known, during the long European odyssey of the Jewish people, is *shul*—from the old Greek word *scola*, or "school." Worship and study were thus combined in the synagogue itself, which was not just a "house of worship" but also for many long centuries a place of disciplined, communal study. As the Talmud enjoins, "Actual learning is accomplished only in the company of others."[20] In the *shul* the students, like their ancestors among the Sons of Light, would drift from one

group to the next, reading, reciting, arguing. They vocalized
their studies in melodious warble. In their ardent singing they
were conveyed to a world beyond, one of exhilaration and en-
chantment. However dreary their environs might be, the rabbis
and their students always found escape in a world of study, a
world of ecstasy. In Jewish tradition, study has always been the
highest form of worship. It is a legacy owed at least in part to
the tradition of the ancient Essenes.

We can only imagine what entering the world of the Sons
of Light must have been like. We have no direct description of
the study practices of the Many among the Secret Scrolls, but
they likely resembled those found in later Jewish tradition. A
memoir of an old European house of study—a *yeshiva*—where
a pietistic movement called *Musar* ("moral instruction") was
employed, gives us a hint of some very ancient practices. One
can almost imagine the Overseer of the Many and the Teacher
of Righteousness in the figures of the "Supervisor" and the
"Edifier" described as follows:

> *A visitor entering the large hall ... could see the Supervisor mov-
> ing like a shadow among the diligent students. But everyone
> knew that he and his authority were not of the essence there. The
> authority of Musar ("moral instruction"), and the Edifier, who
> wielded the authority, played the essential role. Rabbi Netta
> Hirsch Finkel ... called "the Grandfather," would go around the
> yeshiva in seeming humility. But all knew that the power and
> rule were vested in him. ... [He] would look around constantly
> as if searching for something in the behavior of the students that
> was not to his liking or taste. Sometimes he would stop beside
> the desk of a yeshiva youth and examine his comportment—his
> chanting, his movements, his reactions to what was going on
> around him. The youth upon whom Rabbi Netta Hirsch fixed*

*his stare would shake with fear before the penetrating gaze, un-
certain as to whether he had found favor and approval in the
eyes of his examiner. Rabbi Netta Hirsch stood in the center of
all that went on in the yeshiva, and yet stood above it all.*[21]

The Gods of Knowledge

No one could possibly dominate the Sons of Light nor
could anyone control them, as long as their minds were free. Let
the Romans and their puppet monarchs, the dynasty of King
Herod, rule Jerusalem and Judea. They would not rule over the
society of the Many. Indeed, King Herod and his heirs established a "bureaucracy" of unparalleled brutality, wherein any
and all opponents mysteriously disappeared and where the entire population lived in fear. Intimidation was the rule in a realm
where people's very minds were whipped into submission.

By contrast, the desert settlement of the Essenes, nestled in
splendid isolation by the lake of death, was a citadel of freedom—the freedom of the mind. So has it been throughout
human history, for tyrants have never been able to enslave those
whose minds are unfettered. As the scroll of *Blessings* declares:

> *May the Eternal lift you up, setting you upon infinite heights.
> May you be like a strong tower, perched atop a high wall....
> May you be granted the spirit of counsel and everlasting
> power—a spirit of knowledge, along with the fear of the Eternal.*
> —BLESSINGS (1QSB), col. 5:23, 25

Knowledge is dynamic; knowledge is a fortified tower.
Learning is the path to its attainment. Study was the way,
along which the feet of the Many trod, in the trackless wilderness they called home. The end and by-product of this path
was the apprehension of the mysteries of the universe.

The Secret Scrolls have some incredible things to say about those with true knowledge. The strange mystical document called the *Song of Sabbath Sacrifices* is one of the most enigmatic texts ever unearthed. Discovered in fragments in both the caves of Qumran and atop the rocky promontory in the Judean wilderness known as Masada, it is a font of the mystical discipline called Kabbalah, in this case consisting of a series of songs uttered by the angels on high. It is an angelic liturgy, accompanying the celestial sacrifices offered in the spiritual temple in the ethereal realm. The divine beings intone praise; the scroll transcribes their words. And the words recorded refer to certain beings with true knowledge (whether human or supernatural is unclear) as "gods":

> *In the community of all the "gods" of knowledge—and in the assemblies of all the divine spirits—the Eternal has engraved ordinances for all works of the Spirit. Judgments of glory are engraved for all who establish true knowledge—a people with the knowledge of God's glory. They are the ones closest to eternal knowledge—to the fountain of holiness....*
> —SONG OF SABBATH SACRIFICES (4Q400), frag. 1, col. 1:4–7

Elsewhere, the scroll intones:

> *Hallelujah to the God of everlasting heights! Give praise, you exalted ones, among all the "gods" of knowledge!*
> —SONG OF SABBATH SACRIFICES (4Q403), frag. 1, col. 1:30–31

Imagine being godlike, being transmuted, individually, into the image of deity, holy and incorruptible. This is an idea that captivated the ancients and which underlay a good deal of ancient mythology, from the Greek isles, to Babylonia, to the Nile Valley, where the pharaohs were thought to be transmuted into immortal deities at the time of their entombment. Who, among the sons of men, did not aspire to attain the power of the gods? The Sons of Light, however, had a different idea about deity. According to the Essenes, it was not divine power per se that characterizes the image of God, but divine wisdom and divine knowledge. They conceived of the Eternal as being all powerful but also all wise and all just. This was a fundamental difference between the Essenes' deity and the gods of the pagans. Their gods may have been conceived as omnipotent, ruling over the elements, the sun, the rain, the waters. But they were also thought to be generally capricious, given to whim and fickle emotion. The same gods who sent rain in its season also withheld it, causing deadly droughts; or they may have decided to inundate the land in violent floods.

The God of the Sons of Light, however, was believed to stand above nature. With wisdom and justice added to might, their God judged the world in righteousness. Life was not perceived as unfolding haphazardly or by fickle chance, for justice pervades the cosmos. It is an audacious thing to believe, especially going into the twenty-first century (in light of the terrors produced in the twentieth), that things happen for a reason. But such a perspective is an aspect of attaining wisdom and knowledge.

Are the "gods of knowledge" supernatural beings who attend in the divine court on high? Or is this a description of the covenantal community—of those who have joined the Sons of Light? In any case, it is knowledge, rather than might and power, which the Essenes believed to be the greatest measure of godliness. And their knowledge was, of course, a function of their study. The angelic liturgy further declares:

> *They are to tell of the glory of the divine kingdom, according to their knowledge.... In all the highest heavens, and in all the*

everlasting heights, they are to extol the divine wonders, accord-
ing to all their wisdom and understanding.
—SONG OF SABBATH SACRIFICES (4Q400), frag. 2, 3–4

Compare the "gods of knowledge" with the Omnipotent
One, who rules over all by the power of knowledge:

From the God of knowledge proceeds everything that has ever
existed. From the plans of the Eternal are all things eternally
established.
—SONG OF SABBATH SACRIFICES, Masada Fragment (4Q402),
frag. 4:12–13

In Your eternal wisdom, everything has existed, from the begin-
ning. Even before creating them, You knew the deeds of all Your
creations, forever and ever.
—PSALMS SCROLL, col. 9:7–8

The Sons of Light believed that it is knowledge, the knowledge possessed by a supreme intelligence, which brought the
world into being. It is knowledge that sustains all things, integrates all things, harmonizes all things. As one contemporary
scholar and critic observes, "The universe is the product of intelligence and aim; in the absence of intelligent organization of
a thousand details vast and small, we would not exist."[22]

The Sons of Light were also told of the role of divine
knowledge, filling the universe with light and banishing gloom,
in the precise order of the cosmos:

The divine dwelling consists of pure light. All gloom and haze
vanish in the divine presence.... The sons of Adam have been set
apart—with light from the sun during the daytime, and moon-

light and starlight by night. Indeed, the Eternal is suffused with
light, impenetrable, unknowable light.

—A LITURGICAL WORK (4Q392), frag. 1:5–7

The Seven Sovereign Princes

The *Song of Sabbath Sacrifices* heaps great accolades upon
those who have attained true knowledge. It envisions a series
of seven angelic "princes," who employ groupings of seven
mystical words, blessing those whose diligent study has
brought them wisdom.

The first among the Cardinal Princes is to bless—in the glorious
name of the Eternal—all those who have attained great knowl-
edge—with seven words of wonder. He will bless the ones who
have learned everlasting things. . . .

The second among the Cardinal Princes is to bless . . . everyone
who exalts the eternal King—with seven words of wondrous
glory, all pure from eternity. . . .

The third among the Cardinal Princes is to bless—in the name of
the exalted kingdom—all who are raised up with knowledge—
with seven words of exaltation. . . .

The sixth among the Cardinal Princes is to bless—in the name of
the divine spirits—all who are strong in knowledge. . . .

The seventh among the Cardinal Princes is to bless—with seven
words of wondrous holiness—all the holy ones who lay a foun-
dation of knowledge. He will bless all those who exalt the divine
ordinances with seven words of wonder—which will be for them
as impenetrable shields.

—SONG OF SABBATH SACRIFICES, Masada Fragment (4Q403), frag. 1,
col. 1:10–14, 21, 23–25

Seven is a mystical number, used throughout the biblical text to suggest perfection and completion—the undiminished harmony of the created order. We do not know who the seven princes are or how they rank in the supernatural hierarchy, but they certainly echo the prevailing theme of this mystical liturgy—the concept of might and power *through* wisdom and knowledge.

Repeatedly the angels above extol those below, among mortals, who by their study have gained wisdom and counsel. While the angels are supernatural in stature, those who have gained knowledge are at least on an equal footing:

> *Celebrate—all you who delight in divine knowledge! Rejoice among the "gods" of wonder! Declare the glory of the Eternal with the tongue of all who disseminate knowledge. Wonderful praise fills the mouth of all who bring forth knowledge. Indeed, the Eternal rules over all who celebrate eternal knowledge—all who judge, through divine strength, all the spirits of understanding. Offer thanksgiving—all you "gods" of majesty—to the King of majesty. For all the "gods" of knowledge praise the divine glory. All the spirits of righteousness extol the divine truth. They try to make their knowledge acceptable, according to the divine decrees.*
>
> —SONG OF SABBATH SACRIFICES (4Q403), frag. 1, col. 1:36–38

Study, more than any other discipline, preserved the people of Israel across the centuries, providing a bulwark against every external force that warred against them. The domain of the mind was also seen as the domain of spirit. For the Sons of Light, this was reality; everything else was illusion:

> *Glory is to be found in the pure light of knowledge—in all the sanctuaries of wonder.*
>
> —SONG OF SABBATH SACRIFICES (4Q403), frag. 1, col. 1:45–46

The Holy of Holies

Researchers today are fascinated with the arrangement of the ancient Temple, decked with a profusion of gold, that stood prominently in Jerusalem. The inner sanctum, where no one save the high priest was allowed to enter and even he only on the Day of Atonement, was called the Holy of Holies. It was the chamber wherein the famous Ark of the Covenant rested in dazzling glory. But for all the discussion about the physical layout of the great Temple and the whereabouts of the mystical Ark of the Covenant, the Sons of Light, in their ancient angelic liturgy, insisted on linking knowledge with the Most Holy Place, and words of knowledge with the sacrifice upon the altar. Writing of the celestial temple, the invisible counterpart of the great building in Jerusalem, they proclaimed:

> *Offer thanks to the God of gods, you seven priests of the Holy of Holies ... through an exhaustive knowledge of the seven regions of the Inner Sanctuary.... The tongue of the first will be strengthened seven times by the tongue of the second. The tongue of the second will be strengthened seven times by the tongue of the third. The tongue of the third will be strengthened seven times by the tongue of the fourth.... The tongue of the seventh will be strengthened by the Holy Sanctuary itself.*
> —SONG OF SABBATH SACRIFICES (4Q403), frag. 1, col. 2:20, 23–29

In the same vein we are told that knowledge is one of the essential ingredients in purification for service in the temple's inner sanctum:

> *The figures of glory—of the marvelous Inner Sanctuaries—spirits of eternal "gods"... are made pure with salt. They are spirits of knowledge, truth, and justice, in the Holy of Holies.*
> —SONG OF SABBATH SACRIFICES (4Q405), frag. 19:2–4

The details of the divine temple service are also delineated, wherein ethereal winged beings called cherubim are envisioned, extolling the "God of knowledge." Bear in mind that what transpires in the physical temple is believed to be merely a reflection of the divine sanctuary. But the keys to the doors of both are the qualities of wisdom and knowledge:

> *Hallelujah to the God of ... marvels. ... Magnify the name of*
> *the Eternal—according to the glory in the tabernacle of the*
> *God of knowledge. The cherubim fall down before the Eternal*
> *and utter blessings. When they arise, the still, small voice of*
> *God is heard.*
> —SONG OF SABBATH SACRIFICES (4Q405), frag. 20, col. 2–21–22:6–8

Who is worthy to enter the sacred precincts? The Secret Scrolls tell of the "gods of knowledge" in the celestial temple:

> *When the "gods" of knowledge come in through the doors of*
> *glory ... the doors of entrance as well as the gates of exit will*
> *declare the glory of the King.*
> —SONG OF SABBATH SACRIFICES (4Q405), frag. 23, col. 1:8–9

As the heavenly liturgy continues, we are told yet more about the seven supernatural princes:

> *The Princes who oversee the praise-offerings possess tongues*
> *of knowledge. They bless the God of knowledge for all*
> *the works of glory.*
> —SONG OF SABBATH SACRIFICES (4Q405), frag. 23, col. 2:12

The Sons of Light were always to remember, that the knowledge they gained was not for their own benefit but a call to service and to action—to be harnessed in the repair of the world. Another brief text, a manual of "blessings," links the imagery of the Holy of Holies with illuminating the world. Knowledge is not only power; it is light to the nations. For the Sons of Light, it was their clothing, their daily raiment:

> *May you be made holy among the people of the Eternal. May you be like an everlasting light, making the whole world shine with knowledge. May you light up the face of the Many. May you be a diadem in the Holy of Holies!*
> —BLESSINGS (1QSb), col. 4:27–28

An additional small document called *The Triumph of Righteousness* gives voice to the greatest longing of the ages, that human beings might one day conquer base, animal instincts that have driven the species to the brink of self-annihilation. The prophetic tongue of the scroll declares:

> *Knowledge will fill the whole world, and there will be no folly anymore.*
> —MYSTERIES (1Q27), frag. 1, col. 1:7

Woe to Hypocrites!

Remember, however, that the acquisition of knowledge was not an abstraction; it was practical. It was essential that the Sons of Light act upon the things they studied, incorporating each principle into their lives. They were to allow knowledge to transform their behavior. Above all, they were to be consistent and congruent with the truth they discovered:

> *You should not attempt to learn a precept from a hypocrite. . . . You should not approach a furnace with one who totters, because he might melt like lead, being unable to resist the flame. . . .*
> —A SAPIENTIAL WORK (4Q424), frag. 1:4–5

On a practical level, the members of the community were told:

> *Never allow [one who judges first and investigates later] to oversee those who pursue knowledge. . . .*
> *Never commission a blind man to bring a vision to the righteous. . . .*
> *Never dispatch an ignorant person to mine new ideas, because the wisdom within him is hidden. He will be unable to rule his own heart. . . .*
> *But a wise person will acquire true wisdom. A righteous person will find delight in reasoned judgment. . . .*
> *He will be a bulwark against all those who dismantle righteous boundaries.*
> —A SAPIENTIAL WORK (4Q424), frag. 3:1–3, 6–9

Their path of study was holistic. As opposed to the fragmented approach of modern Western society, it was an integrated process that saw all aspects of life as interconnected. The Sons of Light could not learn physical disciplines without learning metaphysical disciplines. They could not appreciate the natural without apprehending the supernatural. For the metaphysical world is like the root system that supports and nourishes the tree. Therefore their study was to be no more fragmented than their lives. Their very thoughts were to proceed from the knowledge of their hearts:

> *In the beginning of each and every thought, there is a heart of knowledge—and the offering that comes forth from righteous lips—made ready for all true worship.*
> —SONGS OF THE SAGE (4Q511), frags. 63–64:3–4

Know Thyself

Einstein once commented that among the things that appealed to him most about his cultural heritage was the pursuit of knowledge, not for some utilitarian purpose but for its own sake:

> *The pursuit of knowledge for its own sake, an almost fanatical love of justice, and the desire for personal independence—these are the features of the Jewish tradition which make me thank my stars that I belong to it.*[23]

But study is about much more than knowledge in the abstract; it leads to self-knowledge. When we study, we find a certain internal connectedness; we get in touch with ourselves, our humanity, the essence of our being. Study authenticates us. In accruing knowledge, we discover who we are. The story is told of an old Hasidic master, Rabbi Zusya, who once observed, "If I am asked in the world to come why I was not Moses, I will know what to answer. But if I am asked why I was not Zusya, I shall have nothing to say."[24]

7 Perseverance:
The Steadfast Soul

I LEARNED FREEDOM OF WILL AND *undeviating steadiness of purpose; and to look to nothing else, not even for a moment, except to reason.*

—Marcus Aurelius,
MEDITATIONS, Book I, 8

NEVER GIVE IN, NEVER GIVE IN, NEVER, *never, never, never—in nothing, great or small, large or petty—never give in except to convictions of honor and good sense.*

—Winston Churchill, 29 October 1941,
Harrow School, United Kingdom

◇◇◇◇◇◇◇◇◇◇◇◇◇

T HE DESERT is relentless and unmerciful, like the surface of the moon, or some other distant, alien world. The blazing sun gives no quarter. The desert is what it is because it is persistent in its harshness. Moreover, the only living things that thrive here are those that are perfectly adapted to this severity. The creatures of the desert seem to be in tune with this cadence, from scorpions to lizards to snakes. Life will find a way because of the doggedness of living things. To learn persistence, come to the desert.

A Matter of Survival

Deserts are an amazing aspect of the earth's topography. Rising masses of air from tropical latitudes lose their moisture by condensation, producing tropical rain forests on either side of the equator. But these same masses of air, now rid of their water particles, descend into subtropical regions, resulting in high pressure zones, where any and all moisture in the lower atmosphere is absorbed. Any trace of cloudiness dissipates and vanishes, and intense solar radiation mercilessly blankets the ground. Of all the myriad forms of plant and animal life that call the desert their home, human beings are the least adapted for survival. Humans have no special organs for storing water. Frail and defenseless, a human being's chances of surviving even a single day alone in the wilderness are nonexistent. Unless shelter is found, a typical human in the desert loses between four and six pints of water in the morning hours alone. By evening a staggering fifteen pints evaporate away through the pores. Across the centuries, a great many travelers have died along the caravan routes, from the lush "Promised Land" in the west to the boundless tracts of sand called the Arabian Desert in the east. Surviving in this wasteland is a daily, life-and-death struggle.

"In the desert," wrote Isaiah of old, "prepare the way of the Lord." Imagine the persistence of character, the steadfast purposefulness needed by the Essenes of the Judean wilderness. Imagine the cadence of their daily existence, once having taken up the cause of this particular order. The goal demanded a dis-

cipline and a consistency foreign to many modern people. The
Secret Scrolls, however, do not mince words in propounding
their ancient virtues. They lay out the requirements in no uncertain terms.

Of the Sons of Light the ancient historian writes these
laudatory words:

> *They contemn the miseries of life, and are above pain, by the*
> *generosity of their mind.*
> —Josephus, WARS, II, VIII, 10

The sacred constitution of the Essene library says it equally
well:

> *All who enter into the Covenant of the Eternal—who accept the*
> *Manual of the Community—are to do everything commanded of*
> *them. During all the dominion of the Evil One, they are not to*
> *turn aside or stray, due to fear, horror, or torment.... They are*
> *not to depart from any of the precepts of truth, veering neither*
> *to the right nor to the left.*
> —MANUAL OF DISCIPLINE, col. 1:1–18

Truly, the fears, terrors, and afflictions of the wilderness of
Judea are multiple, which is why a very special determination
was required.

The great rule book also admonishes:

> *Whoever comes into this covenant—yet venerates the idols of*
> *his own heart—will be cursed. Such a person sets up in front of*
> *himself a stumbling block—forged from his own iniquity—only*
> *to trip over it.*
> —MANUAL OF DISCIPLINE, col. 2:11–12

There is nothing like the desert for demolishing idols of the
heart, for utterly diminishing in perspective the material things

that distract us, rob us of vision, and divert us from the path on which we must walk. Life is a journey, and only those who walk its path with fidelity experience its joy and rapture in counterpoint with its occasional turmoil. The image of "tripping" as opposed to "walking" suggests this, and the image of "iniquity" as a "stumbling block" is equally telling. Victory goes not to the strong but to the persistent. The Community Rule continues:

> *Although a person hears the words of this covenant, he only flatters himself in his own heart. He declares, "Peace be upon me, in spite of the fact that I walk in the stubbornness of my heart." Nevertheless, his spirit will be annihilated—without exoneration—for it is parched and thirsty, yet moist (with deception).*
> —MANUAL OF DISCIPLINE, col. 2:13–15

Images from the desert pervade this passage. The lack of truth is equated with being parched and desiccated, and the spirit of smugness and complacency, which says, "Peace be upon me," may appear as the blessedness of water but amounts only to deception. But there is another kind of water in this desert of the soul. The sacred constitution calls it the "spirit of true counsel," by which all sins are expiated and by which one may "look squarely at the light of life."[25] Spiritual victory comes via a unique combination of illumination on the one hand and humility on the other:

> *Once his flesh has been cleansed—by being sprinkled with the waters of purity—he will be sanctified through the waters of repentance. He will humbly submit his soul to the ordinances of the Eternal.*
> —MANUAL OF DISCIPLINE, col. 3:8–9

A kindred religion of the Near East, Islam, operates by the maxim "Purity is half the faith." So it was among the Sons of Light, as they continually purified themselves in plaster-covered ritual immersion baths. The truth, according to the members of the covenant, was deceptively simple. Victory demands perseverance, and perseverance means attaining purity, walking the path, straying neither left nor right. Of course, paths are easily discerned in the desert, where the sparseness of the terrain makes visible even the faintest of trails. Alternatives are easily perceived. "The Eternal has created human beings to govern the world," declares the rule book, which goes on to say:

> *The Eternal has placed within human beings two spirits, in which to walk until the time of the divine visitation. They consist of the spirit of truth and the spirit of deceit.*
> —MANUAL OF DISCIPLINE, col. 3:17–19

Addicted to Virtue

The Secret Scrolls declare the attributes that must be instilled in your heart as you walk ahead on the road called perseverance:

> *... a spirit of humility, of patience, and overflowing compassion, of everlasting goodness, of intelligence, of understanding, of an authoritative wisdom which trusts in all the deeds of the Eternal—which leans on divine lovingkindness—a spirit of the knowledge of every divine act, of zeal for righteous judgments, of holy thought with a steadfast soul.*
> —MANUAL OF DISCIPLINE, col. 4:3–5

A persevering soul, learning endurance in the desert, can be no stranger to humility. The desert itself strips you of pride and pretense. For much of the year the blistering heat precludes serious labor during all but the morning hours, and whatever great exertion is to be performed must be carried out incrementally. Great patience is therefore a must for the Sons of Light, whether in tilling the soil—as was done several kilometers to the south of Qumran, at a place known today as Ein Feshka—or in the construction of the settlement itself. The cutting of limestone and moving of the blocks was a long, arduous process, and the patience taught thereby is one of the greatest of the lessons of the desert.

The desert further taught the Sons of Light to persistently balance reason with intuition, intelligence with "authoritative wisdom." As they wended their way along desert paths, reason and intuition, coexisting in delicate balance, led them on to wise action, the accomplishment of mighty deeds by a "steadfast soul." The measure of their deeds was their holy intent, as witnessed by their perseverance. Walking the desolate terrain taught them to place one foot before the other, consistently, mechanically, until exertion became force of habit. Life in this desolate place teaches that the greatest value isn't in the sheer amount of work done but in how much of value is accomplished; and accomplishment, in this brutal terrain, means doing a little bit consistently. Perseverance is addiction—to virtue. Thus, Josephus writes of the ancient order:

> It also deserves our admiration, how much they exceed all other men that addict themselves to virtue, and this is righteousness: and indeed to such a degree, that as it hath never appeared among any other men, neither Greeks nor barbarians, no, not for a little time, so hath it endured a long while among them.
>
> —Josephus, ANTIQUITIES, XVIII, I, 5

"Addicted to virtue" well describes the Essenes' way of life. But like the sparse vegetation that tenaciously clings to life in the great rift valley, certain adaptations were required. The desert shrubs, for example, send long and well-developed roots into the ground, enabling them to grip the face of the chalky marl hills and to extract life-giving minerals and moisture from the earth. For the Sons of Light, it was a matter of sinking their own roots into the fertile soil of their sacred texts. From them they extracted the tenacity required to fashion and to maintain a life of virtue.

The Adversary

The rhythm of a disciplined life, in a multitude of particulars, is what the Secret Scrolls mandate. Just as muscles grow by exerting themselves against pressure, so the Sons of Light grew strong by the force of conflict. The scrolls delineate the ordinances for daily life and then declare:

> *This is how they are to act, year by year, during all the days of the dominion of the Evil One.*
> —MANUAL OF DISCIPLINE, col. 2:19

The presupposition is that inasmuch as the "Evil One" perseveres, so must the Many. But what is this "dominion of Satan" of which the Community Rule speaks?

Long ago in ancient Israelite days, the Hebrew scriptures spoke of an "Evil One" or an "adversary"—a Satan—who frustrates righteous designs and mires the feet of the godly. The book of Chronicles mentions a Satan, a spiritual adversary who "stood up against Israel and incited David to take a census of the Israelites" (1 Chronicles 21:1). The book of Job depicts a courtroom scene of sorts, wherein Satan, an adversary, is among the "sons of God" who come to present themselves before the Lord. It is this adversary, this Satan, who is given charge by God to afflict and torment Job, a righteous man who has consistently lived uprightly.

The prophet Zechariah also mentions an adversary, a Satan, standing before the Lord's angel to accuse the high priest Joshua. The high priest is struggling to encourage the Jews of Jerusalem, who have returned from Babylonian captivity to rebuild their ruined sanctuary. The Adversary seeks to frustrate his work. It is clear that in biblical days Satan was not a proper name (as it later came to be used) but merely a description of any being, visible or invisible, who stands in the way of the divine will. But later generations would develop a complex folklore about this adversary, raising many questions about how Satan was to be understood. Was this a unique spiritual entity, doing battle with the Eternal? Was it some kind of "anti-God," the wicked counterpart of the righteous deity, ruling in hell? Was this a supreme evil spirit, some kind of impersonal spiritual dynamic, loose in the universe? Or was this simply the "evil inclination" in human beings themselves, that part of the human spirit which tends toward evil? Some sages of old even came to think of Satan as each individual's personal struggle with his or her own ego. However the figure of Satan was understood by the Sons of Light, there was a sense that Satan possessed a rule, a dominion, and that this evil dominion held sway in human society. Evil endures; evil perseveres. As long as the dominion of "Satan" endures, as long as human beings are ruled by self-interest and propelled by their own egos, as long as great evil is unleashed and perpetuated on the surface of the earth, so too must the righteous endure and persist in an ongoing struggle against it. But how is this struggle expressed, and what characterizes it?

War

An important aspect of perseverance was the idea that the Essenes' ongoing inner struggle would one day manifest itself in a much larger conflict between the forces of good and evil. They had been called "ministers of peace." Yet, paradoxically, their scrolls prophetically speak of a most frightful war, soon to be unleashed upon all the inhabitants of the land. True labor is one example of what Islam would later call the "greater jihad." Military conflict, however, is an outworking of the "lesser jihad," a "holy war" in defense of righteousness. The Sons of Light believed they would engage one day in a huge "directed struggle," a jihad of sorts, to put an end to oppressive tyranny. The war to come may be properly understood as a moral exercise, the outward corollary of the discipline of the soul. This theme of exertion in the way of the Eternal dominates the writings of the sect. The desert community composed a great war rule, which describes how:

> . . . *the Sons of Light will strengthen themselves in battle to strike down wickedness.*
> —WAR SCROLL, col. 1:13

The document goes on to describe a great apocalyptic war to come. It is an incredible grand finale to history, played out on the desert's vast stage. The Secret Scrolls, in speaking of this time of great trial at some point in the future, describe a world convulsed in agony:

> *This will be a period of terrible tribulation. It will come upon all the people whom the Eternal has redeemed. Among all of their trials, nothing will be as terrible as this—hastening toward the end—toward everlasting redemption.*
> —WAR SCROLL, col. 1:11–12

The terrors are great, but the key to victory, in war as in the whole of life, is rugged determination and a dogged tenacity that doesn't flinch in the face of adversity. The Sons of Light, knowing that life and perseverance are equivalent forces in an often hostile universe, were accustomed to this, for the desert taught them that survival involves facing asperity on a daily basis. They were to brace themselves mentally for the task ahead. They expected victory but also anticipated setbacks, even crushing defeats. There is an old saying that reverberated from Judea's ancient limestone hills: God alone rules over the people! This was the thought that motivated the Essene comrades-in-arms as they took up the sword late in the first century of the Common Era to liberate their land from Rome's cruel sovereignty.

According to the scrolls, a series of horrific battles, seven in number, were expected to transpire at the very end of days. The outcome, congruent with the immutable will of the Eternal, had long been prophesied:

> *In the course of three lots the Sons of Light will ... strike down wickedness. In three additional lots, the battalions of the Evil One will fortify themselves, forcing retreat upon the Sons of Light.*
> —WAR SCROLL, col. 1:13–14

Three battles were to be won by the Sons of Light, while a mysterious troupe of enemies, obliquely identified as "the battalions of the Evil One," were to be victorious in three other engagements.

Losses were to be expected, as well as the demoralization of many. Extremity, however, is not the time for surrender. It is a time to tap into something greater than oneself. It is time to energize the divine might within:

> *The hordes of infantry will be sufficient to melt the heart; but*
> *at that time, the might of the Eternal will embolden the hearts*
> *of the Sons of Light.*
> —WAR SCROLL, col. 1:14

The seventh battle shall, according to the prophecy, be waged and won by the Eternal, who shall descend from on high with a whole host of angels and grant final victory to the Sons of Light. When human strength fails, opportunity presents itself for divine right to be established and to make itself known. Much can be endured, as long as there exists an inner confidence that justice will win out in the end, that truth will prevail. We need to believe that the universe is a fundamentally benign place, wherein evil will be vanquished in the ultimate triumph of goodness. Possessing such a faith, the Sons of Light were endowed with a firm and unshakable confidence that all will be put right one day, a faith which in turn provided them a formidable measure of courage for the here and now:

> *During the seventh lot, the strong hand of the Eternal will*
> *utterly subdue the Evil One—along with all the angels of his*
> *dominion and all those who belong to his troupe.*
> —WAR SCROLL, col. 1:14–15

In spite of the militancy of this amazing document, the bulk of the text deals not with blood and gore and the din of battle, but with the spiritual exertion of the self. This is directed exertion, an outward expression of the soul's inner perseverance.

What we find in the *War Scroll* is a sequence of specific spiritual directions, engraved upon a series of trumpets: "the trumpets of summons and the trumpets of alarm." By and large the words written on the trumpets simply describe the desert compatriots as "the called of God . . . the princes of God . . . the army of God . . . summoned by God to the council of holiness . . . the peace of God in the camps of the saints." It is the language of religious ritual, not the language of death and destruction. The words represent the fruit of inner exertion, determination, and endurance. The militancy of the scrolls in general is always cast against the militancy of this inner struggle.

> *You have saved my life from the pit . . . from hungry lions*
> *commissioned to devour the sons of guilt—lions who crunch*
> *the bones of the mighty ones and which guzzle the blood of*
> *the brave.*
> —PSALMS SCROLL, COL. 8:6–7

The war described so vividly in the Secret Scrolls is not a physical conflict as much as a liturgical exercise, orchestrated by priests and joined in by a host of angels, who alight from the heavens to vanquish the power of evil. Yet the coming tribulation is to be a time of distress for the children of Israel, but from this cauldron of strife a purged and holy character and purpose emerges.

Even though the battle is described in religious terms— leading us to interpret it in ways more spiritual than physical— it is clear that the sect believed that the spiritual conflict would one day manifest itself physically. The "greater jihad" will become a "lesser jihad" at some point in the near future. For the Essenes of Judea that day came when the whole province rose in revolt against the Romans—who ruled them as an occupational force—in the year 66 of the Common Era. The Sons of Light joined the rebel cause, believing the Romans to be synonymous with the Sons of Darkness. The battle did not proceed according to plan. Judea lost its bid for independence, and the brave little troupe of Essenes perished in the ensuing conflagration. Nevertheless, the lessons of war they wrote of, meticulously inscribed in their library, have by miracle survived to the present day.

Expecting Tribulation

Endurance plans for hardship. As with every military campaign, so it is with life. The parallels are inescapable. Any military strategist begins with a plan, delineating in detail how a particular operation is supposed to proceed. The next stage in planning, however, is to anticipate how the plan will unfold when things go awry, knowing that things will always go at least somewhat differently than what was originally envisioned. The true strength of a leader comes in working through and beyond the unanticipated turns in the road. Such is the secret of perseverance.

For the Sons of Light, anticipating the conflict ahead, the prophecy declares:

> During the thirty-three years of the war that lay ahead, the people of renown—the ones called to the great assembly—along with all the heads of the leaders of the community—are to select mighty warriors, among all the lands of the nations. They will provision gallant soldiers for their defense—from among all the tribes of Israel—to go out to do battle, year by year, according to the rules of warfare.
> —War Scroll, col. 2:6–8

There is a sense here that the final war—now manifest as a physical conflict—will rage beyond the confines of the Holy Land, engulfing other nations as well. It will be a "war to end all wars," a "messianic" war, ushering in a new age of universal peace and brotherhood. The ancient prophecies of Isaiah (thought to be consigned to the end of time) will come to pass speedily in the lifetime of the Sons of Light: for the day will come when "the lion will lay down with the lamb," when "they shall beat their swords into plowshares and their spears into pruning hooks; nation shall not lift up sword against nation, neither shall they learn war any more." The Essenes will join with comrades from many nations. The "heads of family" will recruit warriors, "men of renown," who will engage the enemy among "all the lands of the nations." The admonition is not to wait, passively, for the messianic age to dawn one day. It is the responsibility of the Sons of Light to bring in the messianic age. As Jesus of Nazareth once declared, "The Kingdom of Heaven suffers violence, and the violent take it by force."

The Lion of Judah

A modern exemplar of perseverance may be found in an Israeli war hero, a tenacious military man nicknamed the "Lion of Judah." Ariel Sharon, general and political figure in modern Israel, gained his notoriety in 1973, when Egypt and Syria joined forces to attack the state of Israel during the Yom Kippur War. Taken by surprise, Israel's forces were thrown into retreat by the advance of Egypt's Third Army eastward over the Suez Canal. Meanwhile, Syria invaded over the Golan Heights, in a giant pincer movement that had the potential of annihilating the entire state of Israel. Israeli losses were heavy, and the very survival of the nation seemed imperiled. The United States began a massive airlift, to replenish Israeli losses in weaponry and equipment. The Soviets threatened intervention. The United States went to a state of high alert—Defcon 3. Nuclear war became a real possibility.

Endurance turned out, in the end, to be the deciding factor. Ariel Sharon, in command of Israel's armored brigades in the wilderness of Sinai, not only refused to admit defeat; he exe-

cuted a daring counterattack, fording the Suez Canal in the opposite direction, westward, on a series of pontoon bridges, well
to the south of where the Egyptians had originally made the
crossing. Sharon and his tank columns quickly moved north,
along the west bank of the canal, completely cutting off the
Egyptian Third Army. Imminent disaster was turned into a surprising victory. It was a victory that eventually laid the groundwork for a lasting peace between Israel and Egypt, a peace that
endures to this day. Sharon, the "Lion of Judah," not only
saved his nation from impending destruction; he earned for
Israel the grudging respect of the leader of the Arab world,
Anwar Sadat. The peace that exists today between Israel and
Egypt might never have come to pass had this tenacious general not had the audacity to cross the Suez Canal to the west.

Extinction and the Enduring Legacy

The apocalyptic war anticipated by the Sons of Light did
not turn out as prophesied. During the terrible revolt that consumed the land in the late first century of the Common Era, the
response from the city on the Tiber was swift and overwhelm-
ing. Rome's crack general, Vespasian, and his son Titus led
their legions into the land of Israel, spreading blood and fire all
over Galilee, destroying Jerusalem, burning the holy Temple,
and obliterating the little community whom history has called
the Essenes. There was to be no deliverance from heaven. The
covenantal community of Lake Asphaltis was no match for the
mighty Roman legions. Even the measure of their perseverance
was not enough to keep the little community from sliding into
oblivion. Josephus tells the awful tale:

> And as for death, if it will be for their glory, they esteem it better
> than living always; and indeed our war with the Romans gave

abundant evidence what great souls they had in their trials, wherein, although they were tortured and distorted, burnt and torn to pieces, and went through all kinds of instruments of torment, that they might be forced either to blaspheme their legislator or to eat what was forbidden them, yet could they not be made to do either of them, no, nor once to flatter their tormentors, nor to shed a tear; but they smiled in their very pains, and laughed those to scorn who inflicted the torments upon them, and resigned up their souls with great alacrity, as expecting to receive them again.

—Josephus, WARS, II, VIII, 10

Perseverance had been the Essenes' way in life, and it was equally their way in death. But in another way, the Sons of Light were destined to survive their own extinction. For their legacy has surfaced after a long entombment, via their mysterious library, which today we call the Dead Sea Scrolls. Their legacy flourishes, their teachings endure. The desert disciplines they fostered remain an example for all time.

Intimations of Immortality

There was, however, an additional facet of perseverance that fueled the collective psyche of the Sons of Light. It was the notion that not only must individuals persevere, even in the face of death, but that the souls of righteous individuals equally persevere beyond the brief life we live in fleshly bodies. They came to believe that there must be something more—not only an abundant life in the present but also life beyond life for all eternity. The power of this doctrine was one more reason why the members of the covenantal community left the comfort of Jerusalem, where the ruling priesthood (Sadducees, they called themselves) denied the very notion of the hereafter. The tenacity of their spirits, which longed to find release from fleshly woe, found great solace in the desert, seeking to be united with eternity itself. The raw materiality of Jerusalem seemed to hamper this great quest, even as the vast desolation of the Jordan rift valley tugged at the corners of their souls. Josephus, the consummate philosopher-historian, says the following:

> *The doctrine of the Essenes is this: That all things are best ascribed to God. They teach the immortality of souls, and esteem that the rewards of righteousness are to be earnestly striven for.*
> —Josephus, ANTIQUITIES, XVIII, I, 5

The Secret Scrolls, for their part, are clear about the reward for those who persevere:

> *This pertains to the community of the "poor ones." The whole world is to be their inheritance. They will take possession the high mountain of Israel—forever. They will delight in the holy hill.*
> —COMMENTARY ON PSALMS, col. 3:10–11

> *For the Eternal will heal those who are wounded, bring the dead back to life, and pronounce good news to the poor.*
> —A MESSIANIC APOCALYPSE (4Q521), frag. 2, col. 2:12

Forever. The word embodies a promise as old as the Judean limestone. It expresses a hope that sounds naive in the modern age, dominated as it is by philosophies of nihilism. But for the poor, the downtrodden, the suffering, for those who persevere through tribulation, hardship, and deprivation, in this age and in every age, "forever" is a liberating concept. The flesh dies and decays, but the soul perseveres.

The Fate of the Teacher

One final measure of the perseverance of the Sons of Light links the mysterious events of the past with a vision of the future. It has to do with the fate of the founder of the group, a mysterious and mystical figure known as the Teacher of Righteousness, who, at some point in the second century B.C.E., led his followers into the wilderness to found the community they would call home. A good part of his legacy, however, is persecution, for he was pursued by another mysterious figure, simply known as the Wicked Priest, apparently to the city of Damascus. It was there, on the holiest day of the calendar, the Day of Atonement, that the Teacher of Righteousness was slain by the Wicked Priest. The life of the great teacher was suddenly and unexpectedly extinguished. But the scrolls offer the enduring vision of a glorious future, when the Teacher of Righteousness shall return, either physically, or somehow in spirit, residing in the form of the so-called priestly Messiah.

One of the Secret Scrolls (known today as the *Messianic Rule*) presents a stunning vision of a ritual enacted at the end of days. The priestly Messiah—possibly the revived Teacher of Righteousness—will come to the front of the assembled community, joined by his fellow priests from the tribe of Aaron. All will take their seats before him, by virtue of the order of their rank. The priestly Messiah will be joined by the lay Messiah, from the house of David, and before them both the Many will sit at a common table. A "holy communion" ritual (depicted in the scrolls long before Jesus of Nazareth performed his own "Last Supper") will then be enacted. It is to be an elaborate covenantal meal, sanctified by the priestly Messiah, who will extend his hand over the bread and the "new wine." The scroll concludes with the declaration that the Sons of Light are to pro-

very imp' ort'ant ceed in this fashion at every meal where at least ten of them are gathered. The ritual of the communal meal therefore becomes an enduring statement, a declaration of faith in the endurance and glorious future of a redeemed community.

> *Search it out; find it; take hold of it; and retain it!*
> —EXHORTATION TO SEEK WISDOM (4Q185), col. 2:11–12

Whatever your particular vision, the advice of the Secret Scrolls is more than relevant. Find yourself a teacher, a mentor. Learn from your own "teacher of righteousness" whatever you can, and then learn to celebrate your vision. Establish your own rituals to embody it, to rejoice in it, to proclaim it. Learn to shut off the voices that tell you that it can't be done, whether friends, acquaintances, family, or even your own inner reservoir of doubt. Find your own wilderness, where the voices of naysayers are stilled.

My quest

8 Silence and Right Speech:
The Flute of My Lips

As for me, I have remained silent. What more can I say concerning this matter? I have spoken according to my own knowledge—which proceeds only from a clay vessel. But how can I speak at all, unless You open my mouth? How can I understand anything unless You enlighten me?

—Psalms Scroll, col. 17:32–33

WE LIVE in a culture that bombards us with words. Nevertheless, for all the talking going on, one sometimes wonders if anything of substance is being communicated. We wonder, in a sea of political and societal hypocrisy, whether words today mean anything at all. There was a time, for example, when the phrase "I give you my word" meant something almost sacrosanct, but those days are gone. Moreover, the word "love," arguably the most important word in our language, has become so cheapened as to be virtually meaningless.

Consider, by contrast, the philosophy of a little-known, long-forgotten sect of Judeans, far removed from our own world by geographic isolation and by two long millennia. For the Sons of Light, who came to reside near a lake of sulfur and asphalt, a unique reverence for words colored the whole fabric of their lives. They lived by their words, believing till the end that the ideas words contain would sustain them in this life and in the world to come. Words were not to be treated as the raucous babblings of unrestrained souls. Words, if used properly, are holy. They are the very breath of the Eternal:

> *You have created every breath that passes over the tongue.*
> *You know every word it speaks. You have prepared the fruit*
> *of the lips, before a word was ever uttered. You have placed*
> *each word upon its proper line. You have established the*
> *rhythm of every breath of the lips. You have brought forth*
> *line upon line in accord with divine secrets. You determine*
> *each breath, in accord with its measure.*
> —PSALMS SCROLL, col. 9:27–29

The intent of the Secret Scrolls is clear. Be careful what you speak, for the words on your lips are more than just your own. They represent transcendental utterance, the spoken word of eternal Spirit. The idea that the Divine Presence is communicated through mortal speech may sound ingenuous, but it was an essential part of the Essenes' philosophy.

You Are What You Speak

There is a Hebrew term, *davar* (דבר), that was very close to the heart of the Sons of Light. It carries two distinct meanings.

It means "word"—spoken utterance, verbal communication, conveying meaning and intent—the rough equivalent of the Greek term *logos*. However, *davar* also means "thing"—a tangible object of size, dimension, weight, and mass. There is philosophic meaning in this, beyond mere coincidence, for the Hebrew language inherently teaches that words are "things," not pure abstractions. Words have power; words are of substance. They are tangible, and they carry with them their own force. Words not only inspire, they heal. Likewise they carry destructive power. Words can mend, and words can kill. They serve as both salve and weapon. There is therefore no greater charge than to be a custodian of one's words, justly and rightly discerning each syllable, that the awesome power they carry not be misdirected.

In the information age we are so inundated with words that we earnestly crave the silence of the wilderness. From the incessant prattle of the workplace, we rush home to the constant chatter of the television, accompanied all the way by the clamor of our own car stereo. It is deafening, mind numbing. Driving it all is the power of advertising, urging us to consume more and more, to exhaust our resources upon our own lusts. In tandem with the electronic media are the print media, equally driven by the power of advertising.

At our every turn, and wherever we direct our gaze, the verbal messages beckon us, woo us, lure us: Buy, spend, consume! Wherever we travel and in whatever land we may find ourselves, the lexical bombardment is profuse and relentless.

The Dark Side of Speech

The voice of the wilderness is, by contrast, starkly taciturn, given not to verbosity but to silence. The Essenes of ancient

Judea deeply understood the principle of prudent speech, for even in their day, a cacophony of voices preached ease and comfort, opulence, decadence, and empty hedonism. As we have seen, the Secret Scrolls refer to the owners of these voices as "seekers after smooth things." Indeed, words are frequently slippery, treacherous, loose, and smooth. More often they are spoken to obscure, twist, and distort than to convey the truth. The Secret Scrolls declare that the ways of "the spirit of deception" include "a profane tongue."[26] The Sons of Light spoke in their writings of a mysterious character, the "Wicked Priest," who had led a multitude astray by the power of his smooth and slippery words. Consider also other appellations for the Wicked Priest—the "Man of the Lie," the "Scoffer," the "Spouter of Lies," and the "Liar":

> *The treasonous ones, along with the Man of the Lie ... have not believed in the words of the Teacher of Righteousness— words which came from the very mouth of the Eternal.*
> —HABAKKUK COMMENTARY, col. 2:1–3

> *The Preacher of Lies has caused many to stray. He has built a city of vanity with blood. He has established a community with deceit.... He has trained them in acts of fraud.*
> —HABAKKUK COMMENTARY, col. 10:9–11

Another passage (quoted above in chapter 4) is again relevant:

> *The Scoffer ... enticed them to go astray, into a desolate waste-land where there are no paths. He caused the everlasting heights to sink into the abyss. He led the people away from the path-ways of justice. He removed the Boundary, used by our ancestors to designated their inheritance.... For they searched out smooth*

things. They chose illusions. They searched out breaks [loopholes in the Law]. They preferred the comely neck. They called the wicked "just," and they convicted the just.
—DAMASCUS RULE, col. 1:14–16

The "pathless wilderness" is a consummate image of the desert. Deceit is like an illusion of water in an arid place, a delusive chimera of life and vitality. But the Scoffer has led his congregation into a desert without paths, into a treacherous wasteland with no direction and no roads to follow. The Bible has been called a guidebook for the wilderness, and we may imagine that the Sons of Light viewed it that way.

Far from chasing after "smooth things," the members of the covenantal community felt the need to attune their souls by silence and to bridle their tongues through serious discipline. Above all they felt the need to stress truthfulness and an unimpeachable character expressed through one's words. The tongue is like an instrument, which can be made to spout either vulgarity or beauty:

The flute of my lips I will tune to the Eternal's correct measure.
—MANUAL OF DISCIPLINE, col. 10:9

Right speech, then, is learned, as one acquires skill on a flute. If we heed the Secret Scrolls, we know that our lips are the instruments of eternal spirit, and we must tune them with utmost care in order to play the divine melody. In stark contrast with the world around us where obscenity is commonplace, where ridicule is the rule of thumb, where words are weapons, inflicting insult and injury, the legacy of the Sons of Light is a sense of civility and earnest speech. There is no shame in bridling the tongue.

The Fast of Speech

There is in the eastern branch of Jewry a special fast, which occurs on the day before the feast of Passover. It is a fast, not of food or drink, but of words. This day, called *Taanat Dibur,* or "Fast of Speech," is intended to purify the soul prior to the day that commemorates the exodus from Egypt and the journey into the great wilderness of Sinai. Those who fast from speech on this awesome day endeavor to avoid uttering any word at all. Implicit in this ancient tradition, however, is the idea that silence goes hand in hand with wilderness sojourns. As one Dead Sea psalm asks:

> *What words can I speak if You do not open my mouth? How can I answer unless You grant me perception?*
> —PSALMS SCROLL, col. 18:7

A great power of the desert lies in profound silence. There are no throngs of people clamoring to be heard. Save for the tents of desert nomads, pitched far apart along the desolate landscape, there are no people at all. There are no human voices to compete with one another or with the eternal utterance. Whereas the din of noise, the inevitable by-product of human society, clutters the soul and drowns out the intonations of eternity, the desert environment yields an opposite effect. It opens the soul to a resonance with the universe that can be apprehended only in the stillness of an empty terrain. The prophet Hosea once wrote that the divine presence will lure the people of Israel to the wilderness:

> *Behold, I will allure her, and bring her into the wilderness,*
> *and speak tenderly to her. And there I will give her vineyards,*
> *and make the Valley of Achor a door of hope. And there she*

> *shall answer as in the days of her youth, as at the time when*
> *she came out of the land of Egypt.*
> —HOSEA 2:14–15

When humans are quiet, the Eternal speaks. A derivative of the Hebrew word *davar* (meaning "word" or "thing") is *midbar,* which means "desert." The Hebrew language itself seems to teach that the "word" of God (*davar*—דבר) is heard most clearly in the *midbar* (מדבר)—the "desert." This is the concept behind the "Fast of Speech" on the eve of Passover. Human beings refrain from their own words so that they may hear the divine word. The historian Josephus observes the following regarding the Dead Sea sect:

> *Nor is there any clamor or disturbance to pollute their house,*
> *but they give every one leave to speak in their turn; which*
> *silence thus kept in their house appears to foreigners like*
> *some tremendous mystery; the cause of which is that perpet-*
> *ual sobriety they exercise....*
> —Josephus, WARS, II, VIII, 8

How refreshing, considering that contemporary public discourse typically devolves into shouting matches, that the Essenes should legislate speaking in turn, without interrupting. The ancient historian writes:

> *If ten of them be sitting together, no one of them will speak*
> *while the other nine are against it.*
> —Josephus, WARS, II, VIII, 9

The community rule books adds the following stipulations:

It is not permitted for a person to speak while someone else is
still talking. Neither should he speak prior to a higher rank-
ing person. Whoever is asked to speak should do so in his
own turn. In the Congress of the Many, no one—not even the
Overseer of the Many—should utter even a word unless
asked to do so. Any person who has something to say to the
Many—but who does not hold the position of an official
Interrogator in the Community Council—should stand to his
feet. He should say: "I have something to say to the Many."
If they permit him, he is then to speak.
—MANUAL OF DISCIPLINE, col. 6:10–13

The idea that youth should be silent before age may be considered quaint in today's society, but it is certainly at the heart of
ancient wisdom. The Secret Scrolls clearly legislate that those of
lower rank are to hold their tongues before their elders. What
decorum, that the congregation as a whole and its Overseer must
give consent before any member is allowed to speak. Whenever
the congregation is assembled in its council, any member who
wishes to speak must utter the appropriate formula, thereby ask-
ing permission for making his thoughts known.

The Propriety of Speech and the Lost Art of Civility

Aside from the unimpeachable manners cultivated by the
Sons of Light, for which they were widely known, they practiced a remarkable economy of speech, taking care that inap-
propriate language not issue from their lips. The Essenes'
speech did not even contain "curse words." Nor was the name
of the Almighty uttered as profanity. (A little known fact: the
use of the word "God" as a profane expletive did not evolve
until the Middle Ages and later.) Not only was the divine name

not used by way of a curse, it was not used at all, since it was deemed too holy to pronounce. It is a tradition held in Judaism to this day:

> *Any person who has pronounced the divine Name, which is esteemed above all—whether in cursing, or as a result of some trial or mischance, or in any other circumstance ... whether reading a book, or saying a blessing—will be expelled. Such a person will never be allowed to come back to the Council of the Community.*
>
> —COMMUNITY RULE, col. 6:27; 7:1–7

A kindred passage reads:

> *No one is to take an oath by the divine Name, or even by a euphemism for the divine Name.*[27] *One is only to swear by the oath of the "Sons" or by the curses of the Covenant.*
>
> —DAMASCUS RULE, col. 15:1

There is a related universal concept, that the overuse of words cheapens them. So it is with the name of the Eternal. As God cannot be fully fathomed, as the depths of spirit cannot be adequately plumbed, the divine name isn't to be uttered by carnal lips. It is reserved for a place of eternal mystery, ungraspable awe. By extension of this principle, it stands to reason that if you want to influence your society, if you want to be listened to and respected for your wisdom and your sage advice, you might think about learning to speak less, not more. Speak too much, or speak frivolously, and what you say won't be heeded, even when you want to be taken seriously.

It all comes down to choice. Every minute of the day you are faced with the choice of what words, if any, to employ in a given situation. Unfortunately, people often have the idea that they are helpless against their feelings, that they cannot control what they say or how they express themselves. Contemporary culture is replete with such messages, insinuating that literally anything can and should be said, regardless of the consequences to others. Among the Sons of Light, however, words were considered priceless:

> *Foolishness and mendacity will never be heard from my*
> *mouth. Neither will wile or duplicity be detected on my lips.*
> *No, the fruit of holiness will be on my tongue. Profanity will*
> *never be found on it.*
> —MANUAL OF DISCIPLINE, col. 10:21–23

What comes out of our mouths affects reality. Words spoken to a child, a spouse, a friend, or a neighbor create or destroy relationships. Our very words build the universe that we inhabit. This was the Essenes' overarching theory. What we speak reflects our thoughts. If we keep negativity from our speech, then our thoughts themselves will be less negative. Our words are to be well chosen, perspicacious and effective, each one designed to accomplish a redemptive purpose.

The Dead Sea Psalms contain emotive imagery regarding the value of human speech. In some of the most powerful, though hitherto unknown ancient poetry, voice is given to the concept of a divine fountain, a perpetual spring and source of water in this most desolate locale. The fountain image is repeated in a number of places in the Secret Scrolls. Here it is directly connected with personal speech, with individual utterance, with what words *can* be if we dare to ascribe them to a source beyond human ken:

> *You have opened a fountain in the mouth of Your servant.*
> *You have engraved Your secrets on my tongue, in accord with*

Your measuring line. I will speak this knowledge to all Your
creations. I will explain these things to creatures of dust, just
like me.
—PSALMS SCROLL, col. 23:10–12

The image of the fountain is the perfect contrast with the
wasteland in which these psalms were composed. Just as water
is by no means the natural product of the wilderness, neither is
the eternal word the natural product of the simple person. The
Eternal has engraved the word on our tongues, not by hammer
and chisel, but by a "measuring line," determining with great
precision our every syllable. The individual speaks to fellow
"creatures," interpreting things too difficult for fleshly perception. Human speech is transformed, having become a conduit
for conveying infinite mysteries to flesh and blood, to "dust,
just like me." Again, we read:

> *But You, my God, have placed in my mouth what amounts to*
> *an early rain which will water all—a fountain of living water.*
> *The skies will never fail to open. The fountains will never run*
> *dry. They will become an overflowing river—flowing into deep*
> *oceans, beyond searching out. They will surge forth suddenly,*
> *from unknown, secret places. They will be like waters of the*
> *great Flood—for every tree, both the green tree and the dry.*
> —PSALMS SCROLL, col. 16:16–19

Right speech, like healing waters in the desert, feeds life.

Sound and Fury

Members of the covenant community followed a tradition
laid down in the scrolls for expressing censure: to "rebuke" im-
plied using anger for a just purpose, for a redemptive reason—
namely, to help one's fellow become a better person. Rebuke

involves reprimand or castigation, but it must be accomplished not through self-righteous indignation but in an attitude of humility. As the rule book of the Many declares:

> *Let them reprimand one another in truth, in humility, and in lovingkindness toward one's fellow. One is not to speak to his brother in rage, in an attitude of complaining, with callousness, or with an envious spirit of wickedness. One should never despise another in a hard and uncircumcised heart, but should reprove him properly, in that very day.*
> —MANUAL OF DISCIPLINE, col. 5:24–26

Rebuke is contrasted with hatred. It is an anger channeled and funneled into a constructive, efficacious purpose. Therefore, the Son of Light was to discharge his anger on the same day he felt it, lest it become poisonous to his own soul as well as the souls of others. Anger unvented is like a malignancy that, left unexpressed, destroys both its author as well as its object.

To these admonitions other conditions were added. The Son of Light was not to rebuke his fellow in front of the assembled congregation, unless every effort had been made to effectuate a private rebuke. This was to avoid the kind of embarrassment that often accompanies public accusation. Shaming a person publicly has always been a grave offense in Judaism, and the regulations found among the Secret Scrolls are perfectly consistent with the gravity with which this subject was treated. Furthermore, the private rebuke, while designed to avoid general embarrassment, had to take place in the company of others— "witnesses"—who were there to guarantee that the rebuke didn't escalate into something far more serious and more difficult to contain:

> *Indeed, no one is to bring an accusation concerning his comrade before the Many, unless that person is first reproved in the company of witnesses.*
> —MANUAL OF DISCIPLINE, col. 6:1

> *Anyone who belongs to the Covenant, who brings against his comrade an accusation that has not been verified before witnesses—or who brings the accusation in his own rage, or who slanders his accused comrade before the elders—is one who takes his own vengeance. He is one who harbors resentment.*
> —DAMASCUS RULE, col. 9:2–4

There were of course penalties, specified by the community rule book, for those who failed to abide by the admonitions of the Many. Diffidence is preferable to defiance:

> *Anyone who responds to his comrade with an obstinate attitude—anyone who speaks to his comrade curtly, demolishing the relationship he has with him—anyone who disregards the authority of a person of higher rank—has taken the law into his own hands. Such a person is to be punished for a period of a year. He will be expelled from the community during this time.*
> —MANUAL OF DISCIPLINE, col. 6:26–27

These archaic rules seem alien in our individualistic age of wanton self-expression, alternately aggressive and salacious, at the expense of common decency. The force of such admonishments is to sanction the preservation of decorum, the continuance of civility in all interpersonal transactions. It is a lost concept in modern society.

Words and how we use them form the substructure for all interpersonal relationships. Words are the adhesive that holds a society together, and how one uses them, with respect to teachers and elders and all figures of authority, is ultimately revealing about the health of the general culture. Among the Sons of Light, words were clearly used with reverence and awe, which is yet another reason the little desert community persevered and thrived for two long centuries. For those among the covenantal community who misused the power of the word, the penalty was severe: a full year of penance and, by implication, exclusion from the sacred meal of the congregation. Each Son of Light was to be ever watchful, therefore, lest his anger get the better of him. Judgments such as these were always to be kept in mind:

> Anyone who affronts his comrade—intentionally and without good cause—is to be punished for a period of a year. He will be expelled from the community during this time.
> —MANUAL OF DISCIPLINE, col. 7:4–5

> If someone speaks in his own rage against any of the Priests, whose names are recorded in the Book, he is to be punished for a period of a year. He will be expelled—for the good of his own soul—from the pure Meal of the Many. If, however, his outburst was unintentional, he is to be punished for a period of six months.
> —MANUAL OF DISCIPLINE, col. 7:2–3

> Anyone who vents ill will toward his comrade—without good cause—is to be punished for a period of six months to a year.
> —MANUAL OF DISCIPLINE, col. 7:10

The ancient historian also bears witness to the precise details found in the Secret Scrolls regarding the verbal decorum required of the Sons of Light. The modern reader is given testimony of the Essenes' unique ability, cultivated through the years, to channel their anger in an upright and appropriate mode, and to avoid the wanton display of passion that so often hinders the progress of interpersonal growth:

> *They dispense their anger after a just manner, and restrain their passion. They are eminent for fidelity, and are the ministers of peace....*
> —Josephus, WARS, II, VIII, 8

There is another ancient compendium of Jewish wisdom, the Mishnah, that admonishes similarly: "Be of the sons of Aaron, loving peace and pursuing peace . . ." (Tractate *Avot* 1:12). The biblical book of Proverbs tells us: "Life and death are in the power of the tongue" (Proverbs 18:21).

Truth and Consequences

Aside from the problem of anger, there are many other examples of the folly of the tongue, and numerous further proscriptions regarding them are found in the Secret Scrolls. It is written that:

> *Anyone who intentionally tells lies is to be punished for a period of six months.*
> —MANUAL OF DISCIPLINE, col. 7:3–4

The Sons of Light were to speak truthfully at all costs, taking seriously every word they uttered, as though it were said on solemn oath. The admiring attestation of the historian lauds their truthfulness, as though it were a sign of some great and holy dedication:

> *Whatsoever they say also is firmer than an oath; but swearing*
> *is avoided by them, and they esteem it worse than perjury; for*
> *they say, that he who cannot be believed without [swearing*
> *by] God, is already condemned.*
>
> —Josephus, WARS, II, VIII, 8

Jesus of Nazareth was, apparently, similarly impressed, drawing upon this teaching and applying it to his personal disciples:

> *Let what you say be simply "Yes" or "No"; anything more*
> *than this comes from evil.*
>
> —MATTHEW 5:37

The misuse of words—lying—carried with it distinct consequences. One could always rationalize, contrive extenuating circumstances, or simply overlook a lack of truthfulness. But a lie is a lie. The Sons of Light recognized deceit for what it is, and accepted the repercussions that invariably follow. In the covenantal community, those repercussions usually consisted of isolation from the group. This form of penance, as an incentive for ethical conduct, was the strongest sanction of all.

Other admonitions from the community rule book include the following:

> *Anyone who speaks to his comrade deceitfully—or who*
> *intentionally plans to beguile him—is to be punished for a*
> *period of six months.*

> *Anyone who speaks folly from his mouth—three months.*

> *Anyone who interjects his own words while his comrade is*
> *still speaking—ten days.*
>
> —MANUAL OF DISCIPLINE, col. 7:5, 11–12

There was also the matter of untruths spoken to denigrate or slander someone else:

> *Anyone who has a habit of vilifying his comrade is to be expelled from the pure Meal of the Many. He is to be punished in this way for a period of one year. But anyone who goes around vilifying the Many is to be sent away from the community, never again to return.*
> —MANUAL OF DISCIPLINE, col. 7:17–19

The worst form of loose speech is what was referred to as "muttering," namely, a plaintive grumbling and susurration. It may seem relatively harmless, but it reflects the very discontent capable of unraveling any organization:

> *Anyone who mutters against the government of the Community is to be sent away, never again to return. If, however, he mutters only against his comrade—without just cause—he is to be punished for a period of six months.*
> —MANUAL OF DISCIPLINE, col. 7:19–20

Right speech, according to the scrolls, involves transparency and candor before one's extended family, as well as a degree of sworn and dedicated silence before the outside world:

> *And that he will neither conceal anything from those of his own sect, nor reveal any of their doctrines to others, no, not as though anyone should compel him to do so at the risk of his life. Moreover, he swears to communicate their doctrines to no one except those from whom he received them himself....*
> —Josephus, WARS, II, VIII, 7

Jesus of Nazareth declared in the same vein, "Do not throw your pearls before swine, lest they trample them under foot and turn to attack you" (Matthew 7:6).

Actions Speak Louder

Certainly of all freedoms cherished by modern Western society, none is more revered than freedom of speech. People greatly value the right to express themselves openly and in unfettered fashion. Nevertheless, good sense suggests limits, even on the most hallowed of liberties. As Supreme Court Justice Oliver Wendell Holmes once ruled, freedom of speech doesn't entitle a person to yell "Fire!" in a crowded theater. Free speech entails responsibility, and it must be tempered by the exercise of restraint.

With crisp brevity, Voltaire wrote, "Men argue, nature acts." Individuals of course also act, and their actions are infinitely more efficacious than mere aphorisms. For this reason the culture of the Sons of Light always stressed deeds over declarations, acts over utterance. As noted above, one well-reasoned theory for the derivation of the term "Essene" is that it is a corruption of the Hebrew/Aramaic word *Osin,* which means "Doers." This suggests that the Essenes were "doers" rather than "talkers." The scrolls declare:

> *The Community Council . . . consists of the simple folk of Judah—the Doers of the Law.*
> —HABAKKUK COMMENTARY, col. 12:4–5

We also read:

> *All the people will silence their voices . . .*

> *But you, Sons of the Covenant, be steadfast during the trial of God!*
> —WAR SCROLL, col. 17:8–9, 14

The Holy Tongue

An exemplar of the power of the word may be found in a man who, around the turn of the twentieth century, almost single-handedly revived the Hebrew tongue as a spoken, living language. His name was Eliezer Ben-Yehuda. Born in 1858, Ben-Yehuda was a frail, tubercular man, who hailed from the little town of Luzhky in Lithuania but who made his way to Paris early in his life to continue his education. His heart, however, was in the land of Israel, and he was determined, against all medical advice, to immigrate to Jerusalem. The Jewish state was not to be born until 1948, after the Nazi Holocaust, but large numbers of Jews began immigrating in the late nineteenth century as part of the distinctly modern phenomenon called Zionism. From the 1880s on, the numbers of immigrants grew, especially as Jews in eastern Europe experienced greater oppression and sought to escape to their ancient homeland.

What set Eliezer Ben-Yehuda apart from most other immigrants to Palestine was that he recognized the power of language to forge not just a new nation but also a renewed culture. At the time, the Jewish immigrants who had come to Palestine spoke any number of languages, from Yiddish to Spanish to English. Without a common tongue, he feared there could be no common culture and no new nation. Hebrew—the language of the Bible, the tongue of the prophets, the idiom of the Secret Scrolls, and the vernacular of the Essenes—must be reborn.

Struggling against ridicule, Ben-Yehuda began using Hebrew in his own home, refusing to allow any other language to be spoken. He spoke Hebrew to his friends and neighbors and began distributing a local newspaper in Hebrew. Against all odds, he spearheaded a budding Hebrew-speaking movement, which began to catch on, in spite of the fact that never before in history had a language, effectively "dead" for two millennia, been revived as a living, spoken idiom. There was of course opposition. Especially among the ultraorthodox residents of Jerusalem, there were charges that Eliezer Ben-Yehuda was corrupting the "holy tongue" by daring to use it in the "profane" matters of everyday life.

Another problem was that no one spoke Hebrew as a native tongue; it had to be acquired as a second language, which tainted its use with a certain unnatural quality. The ultimate test came when Eliezer Ben-Yehuda became a father. He declared that his son, young Ben-Zion Ben-Yehuda, should hear not a word of any language in the home save Hebrew. All other languages were banned. If one could not speak Hebrew, one should not speak at all. Indeed, it seemed like an age passed before young Ben-Zion spoke any words of his own, and great anticipation descended on the home, as everyone wondered whether his first utterance would in fact be in Hebrew. The child's second birthday passed, and still he had not said a word. But some time later, when at last he opened his mouth in his first verbal utterance, out came . . . Hebrew. Ben-Zion Ben-Yehuda was the first human being since antiquity to speak Hebrew as his mother tongue.

While the language revived in the Ben-Yehuda home was in every respect an ancient idiom, there were many instances in which modern words—expressing various ideas, concepts, and things that didn't exist in antiquity—had to be coined. On many such occasions, Eliezer Ben-Yehuda would conduct long linguistic searches, from library to library in various cities, looking for cognates in some forgotten Canaanite or Moabite tongue. When all else failed Ben-Yehuda simply took a Hebrew root, such as the word for "air" (*aveer*), added an appropriate ending, and invented a word for a machine that travels through the air—*aveeron,* or "airplane."

What began as a single man's vision soon gained an unstoppable momentum. Within a single generation, Hebrew, a truly ancient tongue, now revived, became the lingua franca of Jewish Palestine—a cultural step essential in the birthing process of the modern state of Israel. One could well argue that without this step, on a cultural level, Israel as a nation-state might never have been born. Such is the power of speech; such is the power of the word. The lesson is simple. Watch your words; reverence your words. Recognize that what proceeds from your mouth isn't just a commotion of syllables, reflecting the random thoughts of our unremarkable lives, but that our speech has force and power and a dynamic of its own, capable of building and molding and shaping the world we inhabit. We are indeed what we speak.

9 Manna:
The Sacramental Meal

EVERYTHING HARMONIZES WITH ME,
*which is harmonious to thee, O Uni-
verse.... Everything is fruit to me which
thy seasons bring, O Nature: from thee
are all things, in thee are all things, to
thee all things return.*

—Marcus Aurelius, MEDITATIONS,
Book IV, 23

E ATING has always been at the very heart of human pleasure. With an almost orgasmic delight, the animal kingdom feeds, as various species devour vegetation and,
ultimately, each other. But only among human beings does the
act of feeding come front and center as an expression of one's
philosophy of life. What and how one eats is a philosophical
statement, each human culture developing its own particular
menu in consort with its fundamental approach to living.

Long ago a philosopher named Epicurus established the
notion that eating, drinking, and making merry ought to be a
way of life in a world where nothing is known for certain but
death and taxes. Developed by the philosophical school known

as the Epicureans, the seeking of pleasure became the goal of life, and one very important means to that end was via the palate. Culinary excess should be emulated, not shunned. Gluttony, declared many ancient Greeks, is virtue, not vice.

The Romans subsequently developed Epicurean excess to an art form. A Roman banquet was an exercise in gluttonous hedonism. Course after monstrous course, from exotic birds to roasted wild boar, would be brought to the table by servants and slaves. The diners would systematically gorge themselves over the course of hours, eating until they could hold no more. Still the food came, enticing the taste buds, yet finding no room in the stomach. The Epicurean Roman answer: Next to the banquet hall stood a special chamber, bare in furnishings, save for a stool, a bucket, and a feather. It was called the "vomitorium." Gluttonous diners, having eaten to the full, discreetly retreated to this chamber, deftly regurgitated, and returned to the banquet hall for more, thus qualifying the Romans as the world's first culture of bulimics.

Our habits of consumption reflect the qualities of our souls. The Sons of Light, who chose to live where brackish brine meets sun-blanched sand, mirrored their souls in their psalms. They also used their psalms to portray those whose lifestyles conflicted with their own:

> The strength of aggressors depends on many indulgences—on abundant grain, wine, and oil. They exalt themselves through their property and their affluence.
> —Psalms Scroll, col. 18:24–25

The Sons of Light were, by contrast, "ministers of peace," eating from a different menu. Of the members of the covenantal community the same psalm speaks:

The righteous are like a verdant tree, growing next to a flow-
ing stream. It yields a crop of leaves and propagates many
branches. They are unique among all the sons of Adam. They
will all become hearty and robust from the land.
—PSALMS SCROLL, col. 18:25–26

Given the dusty desolation that is home to the community, where desert wadis surge only intermittently, the image of the verdant tree, taking its sustenance from rushing streams, stirs and resuscitates the arid soul.

Life and the Lake of Death

The Sons of Light, in stark contradistinction with the excesses of the world around them, gave themselves to a different mode of living. Molded and motivated by their own unique philosophy governing human existence, the Sons of Light came to this desolate wasteland in order to find true meaning in the mysteries of life. There was a healthy dualism of life and death here, which was mirrored in the harsh and unforgiving terrain. For the members of the community it was clear that the essence of life wasn't the pursuit of gluttonous pleasure but of profound metaphysical experience, of being fully alive in this land of death. It was a life that was both worldly and otherworldly, "anthropic" and humanistic, as well as deeply spiritual. It was a philosophy that circumscribed every act and every thought, including the way in which they took sustenance.

About midday the Sons of Light would gather together as a great communal body to consume the day's main repast. But this wasn't just supper. The meal represented the ethereal kinship by which all of them were joined—flesh, bone, and sinew—to the mystical organism of covenantal community.

They recognized in the partaking of food that they were but a drop in life's vast ocean, unique and individually separated from the whole, yet intrinsically one with it, sharing the same substance, matter, and essence. The ritual of the great meal conveyed a sense of continuity within the greater scheme of things and cultivated in each participant a deep sense of responsibility in two dimensions: "vertical" and "horizontal."

In the first dimension, "vertical responsibility," they were linked across time to all the generations who preceded them. Each Son of Light was responsible to his forebears to keep the ancient traditions alive (and their memory with them) in every detail of the liturgical practices performed:

> *Every person is to do the will of the Eternal—in accord with*
> *all the things that You have revealed—from age to age.*
> —MANUAL OF DISCIPLINE, col. 9:13

There was also a "horizontal responsibility," whereby each Son of Light was cognizant of the debt he owed to the community at large, his "extended family," for he had joined his soul to theirs:

> *Every person is to firmly adhere to the Chosen Ones of this*
> *age. This is to be in perfect accord with the divine will, just as*
> *they have been commanded.*
> —MANUAL OF DISCIPLINE, col. 9:14–15

Moreover, according to the Sons of Light, each repast was to be both consecratory and celebratory. With respect to the former, the sense of consecration and awe with which the meal was approached flatly ruled out cupidity and the wanton satisfaction of raw appetite. No, there was much more to this repast than the mere filling of stomachs and the dissipation of pangs of hunger. The meal bestowed upon each individual an inner reservoir of mystical strength and fortitude. For the meal was itself a liturgical act, and consuming it was like making sacrifice at the altar. With respect to the latter, the meal—partaken in the presence of the Many—was to celebrate the goodness of creation and to rejoice in the hidden wisdom with which nature speaks:

> *Through the wonders of Your mysteries You have girded me*
> *with strength. For the sake of Your glory, You have revealed*
> *wonders within me—in the presence of the Many. In this way,*
> *You display Your might among all living things.*
> —Psalms Scroll, col. 12:28–29

Eating and Living

"One should eat to live, not live to eat." These words of French comic dramatist Molière (1622–73) sound wise to most of us, but they create a false choice, suggesting that the only alternative to reveling in gluttony (living to eat) is viewing food as a biological necessity, as a trivial pursuit that merely enables us to get on with the real business at hand (eating to live). By contrast, the desert community of the Many believed not that eating is merely tangential to the real purpose of living, but that eating the covenantal meal is integrally bound up with life itself, part of an intelligent design that forces us to recognize our interdependence with the entire universe around us. Eating, therefore, should not be just a means to an end; it should be, in all its communal grandeur, part of the end in itself. It is a physical embodiment of the unknowable, metaphysical, transcendent reality, as Immanuel Kant put it, the *Ding an sich,* the "thing in itself." The "thing" in this case is a sense of primordial unity with community, cosmos, and Creator.

Connected to Sacred Earth

For the Essenes the communal meal assumed a holy aura. Every meal became a "dress rehearsal" for the messianic age, when all evil shall be redressed and when peace shall flow like a vast river. Each individual, each diner, became a "priest," approaching the table as if it were a holy altar. Consecration and ritual purity were the necessary prerequisites for coming to this altar. First, the Son of Light was to dunk himself in a ritual immersion bath in order to attain a level of purity sufficient to the meal. The ancient historian writes:

> *And after this purification is over, they every one meet together in an apartment of their own, into which it is not permitted to any of another sect to enter; while they go, after a pure manner, in the dining-room, as into a certain holy temple, and quietly set themselves down; upon which the baker lays them loaves in order; the cook also brings a single plate of one sort of food, and sets it before every one of them; but a priest says grace before meat; and it is unlawful for any one to taste of the food before grace be said.*
>
> —Josephus, WARS, II, VIII, 5

"As into a certain holy temple." The idea that dining is a metaphysical experience is quite old, and can be found in many ancient societies. However, save for the rote grace, it is unfamiliar in contemporary Western culture. Nevertheless, for the Sons of Light, the meal was a statement of connectedness with each other, with the bounty of the earth round about, and with the essence of God.

That mention is made of the baker fetching loaves suggests a diet that consisted largely of a variety of wholesome grains. And mention of "a single plate" echoes the unity of spirit that all the diners must have felt, as they dipped their bread into what we may assume was a dish of stew or pottage.

The rule book of the Many elaborates many of the same details as Josephus does, setting forth the philosophy of dining in the context of a larger, overriding concern for the wholeness of life. It also dictates the presence of a priest, whose ceremonial propinquity officially converted each meal into a consecrated assembly, united in metaphysical purpose:

> *Everyone is to eat together. Everyone is to say blessings together. Everyone is to deliberate together. Wherever they might be, if there are ten men—from among the Council of the Community— gathered together, at least one of them is to be a priest. Moreover, when the table has been set—ready for the Meal—and the new wine has been poured—ready for drinking—let the priest extend his hand first. He will bless the firstfruits of the bread and the new wine.*
> —MANUAL OF DISCIPLINE, col. 6:3–6 = 4Q258, frag. 1, col. 2:7–10

For the Sons of Light, the daily meal—while it bears similarities to what Christians would later celebrate as the Eucharist (or the Lord's Supper), presided over by a priest and administered weekly—was much more than a goblet of wine and a small wafer. It was a banquet, a great feast, containing the bulk of the day's nourishment. But its consumption, far from being a rushed, perfunctory biophysical necessity, was filled with sacred design and hallowed purpose. The community rule book emphasizes the utterance of a blessing prior to consuming the first bite. This was not designed to sanctify the food (as if food needs sanctification) but to acknowledge one's inherent connectedness with the produce of the earth and to commend the Creator in all creation:

Before I extend my hand to become hearty and robust from
the luscious things of the earth . . . I will intone blessings for
all the wonders of nature, and I will meditate on the might of
the Eternal.

—MANUAL OF DISCIPLINE, col. 10:15–16

In short, the whole purpose of the blessing was not to hallow food but to hallow the Giver. The historian Josephus continues, describing the conclusion of the daily repast, of which
the Sons of Light would partake in consecrated purity:

The same priest when he hath dined, says grace again after meat;
and when they begin, and when they end, they praise God, as he
that bestows their food upon them; after which they lay aside
their [white] garments, and betake themselves to their labors
again till the evening; then they return home to supper, after the
same manner; and if there be any strangers there, they sit down
with them. Nor is there any clamor or disturbance to pollute
their house, but they give every one leave to speak in their turn;
which silence thus kept in their house appears to foreigners like
some tremendous mystery; the cause of which is that perpetual
sobriety they exercise, and some settled measure of meat and
drink that is allotted to them, and that such as is abundantly
sufficient for them.

—Josephus, WARS, II, VIII, 5

A similar theme is echoed in one of the Dead Sea psalms,
which appears to be the exact text of a communal blessing, uttered in unison by the assembled diners, when the repast had
been concluded:

AN INVITATION TO SAY GRACE AFTER MEALS
The voice of Wisdom is heard—coming from the gates of the

righteous ones. Among the community of the merciful ones,
she sings to those who eat their fill. They speak only of her.
When they drink together—in camaraderie—they meditate on
the instruction of the Most High. All of their words are to
proclaim the power of the Eternal.

—Apocryphal Psalm 154 (11Q5), col. 18:12–14

The awesome message is that an unseen guest occupies a
seat at every table. Her name is Wisdom, who is one of God's
personified attributes. She was born at the very instant of creation; she inhabits the whole cosmos. The consecrated meal is
her abode, her sacred sanctuary, the one place where "they
speak only of her." Shared fellowship at table brings forth "the
instruction of the Most High" and produces a special dynamic—the "power of the Eternal."

Nothing happens without intelligent design, and the daily
communal meals of the Sons of Light were no exception. In the
well-oiled functioning of a large community, the division of
labor was a must. Some farmed the fields, others engaged in
trade, especially of salts and spices mined in the vicinity of Lake
Asphaltis. Still others collected the revenues generated, as well
as the produce of the fields, their task being to administrate the
community and to prepare the meals. The historian writes:

They also appoint certain stewards to receive the incomes of
their revenues, and of the fruits of the ground; such as are
good men and priests, who are to get their grain and their
food ready for them.

—Josephus, Antiquities, xviii, i, 5

The results of all this attention to every detail of the preparation and consumption of these desert victuals included remarkably beneficial health consequences. In spite of the fact

that the daily refection was experienced as a great feast, the food itself seems to have been simple, healthy, and most likely grain based. The ancient historian writes regarding the benefits of their diet:

> *They are long-lived also; inasmuch that many of them live above a hundred years, by means of the simplicity of their diet; nay, as I think, by means of the regular course of life they observe also.*
> —Josephus, WARS, II, VIII, 10

Here in this most unforgiving wasteland the law of entropy had been, if not temporarily suspended, at least slowed down. We marvel about any culture anywhere that happens to produce centenarians, from the steppe lands of Russia to the island of Crete, where the secret of longevity appears to be connected with distinctive characteristics of nutrition. Among the Sons of Light long life is directly related to both lifestyle and the "simplicity of diet."

Harmony

Mark Twain observed, "Part of the secret of success in life is to eat what you like and let the food fight it out inside." The Sons of Light taught that a person's diet is an indicator of the essential harmony, or lack thereof, of his or her life. For a disciplined diet not only goes down well; it contributes to an inner harmony, wherein all things are held in balance and whereby the human machine functions and thrives.

How is such internal and interpersonal harmony expressed —or missed—in the contemporary world? In modern culture, though people often have the potential for the kind of communion enjoyed by the ancients, they are unable to experience it.

Ceremony and ritual have been discarded—or are petrified—and most people ignore the metaphysical value of the shared meal.

Modern studies have shown that those who as children have not eaten at a communal, household dining table four days or more per week, bear a fourfold risk of dying of stroke, heart ailments, and cancer. The Sons of Light had a markedly brighter prognosis for health and longevity than most moderns, and in comparison to the ancient world, this was nothing short of miraculous. In an age when the typical life span was not much beyond forty, the centenarians living near Lake Asphaltis must have seemed like demigods. Living two and a half to three times longer than the norm in those days, it would be the rough modern equivalent of people living upwards of two hundred years!

Of course when it comes to centenarians, everyone wants to know: What, exactly, do they eat? That the Sons of Light cultivated grain as well as grapes from vineyards is evident from their rule book, as is their concern for the ethical and moral treatment of both beast and fowl:

> No one is to sell either clean animals or birds to the gentiles. This is to prevent them from being offered up as sacrifices to their gods. No one is to sell them anything from his granary or from his winepress—not at any price.
>
> —DAMASCUS RULE, col. 12:8–10

Beyond such oblique references in the manuals of the community, there are other foods, specifically prescribed as fit—kosher—for consumption. The great *Temple Scroll,* for example, lists a number of items on the community menu, some of which might shock contemporary palates:

You are allowed to eat . . . the cormorant, the stork, every type
of heron, the hoopoe, and the bat. You are also allowed to eat
various flying insects, including: all types of great locust, all
types of bald locust, all types of crickets, and all types of
grasshoppers. You are allowed to eat the following from among
the flying insects: the ones that walk about on four legs, and the
ones whose rear legs are larger than their front legs, in order to
hop up from the ground and fly.
—TEMPLE SCROLL, col. 48:1–5

The cormorant is a large bird, related to the pelican, which
lives in and around the water. Storks and herons are related to
one another, both equipped with long legs and beaks. Such
birds would have been hunted in the desert oases, which crop
up among the cliffs intermittently, from Jericho to Ein Gedi
(well to the south of the main Essene settlement). The hoopoe,
known for its "hoop-hoop" call, is distinctive for the plumage
on its head—fawn-colored feathers with black tips. The bat is
a quintessential cave dweller, well known to the crevasses
round about the main settlement. Often feared across north
Africa and the Middle East, the "desert locust," or *Schisto-*
cerca gregaria, is the species referred to in the Hebrew Bible
and the Secret Scrolls.

While this passage is largely a reworking of the eleventh
chapter of Leviticus, the foods listed are certainly chosen for a
reason, and may provide some interesting details about the
kind of diet the community was accustomed to. Before being
repulsed at such peculiar fare as bats and locusts, bear in mind
that a great many "exotic" foods are considered genuine deli-
cacies in certain cultures. Consider what another passage, from
a community rule book, has to say:

> *No one is to become defiled through eating an unclean beast or*
> *insect. This includes everything from the larvae of bees to crea-*
> *tures that slither about in the water. No one is allowed to eat*
> *fish, unless they are first cut open, while still living, and drained*
> *of their blood. With regard to various types of locusts, they are*
> *to be plunged into fire or into water while they are still living,*
> *because this is the requirement for their species.*
> —DAMASCUS RULE, col. 12:11–15

From this it is apparent that fish were consumed, in addition to various insects.

What, if any, were the dietary benefits to be derived from this unusual menu? It was a diet conspicuously lacking in red meat and fat, but high in protein. While much of the ancient world delighted in drinking to excess, mixing intoxication with sheer gluttony, the Sons of Light practiced a different way. For the sake of healthful sobriety, common table wine, prevalent in the world beyond, was replaced with so-called new wine, or *Tirosh*. It was the unfermented fruit of the vine, juice from the grapes grown in the community vineyard. As noted earlier, a special feast day had been added to the liturgical calendar, in honor of this most important beverage:

> *They are to consume the wine, from the Feast Day of the*
> *New Wine to the following Feast Day of the New Wine—of*
> *the next year.*
> —TEMPLE SCROLL, col. 43:7–9

Drunkenness and the abuse of alcohol of any variety was unheard of among the Dead Sea community. When life itself is an expression of joy and peaceful sobriety, it needn't be clouded with alcoholic stupor. Little wonder that the historian would marvel at "that perpetual sobriety they exercise." Moreover, the medicinal benefits of grape juice (in addition to or in place of wine) consumed in significant quantity are only now being appreciated, and the medical community has finally come around to recommending several glasses of grape juice a day—unlikely for moderns but a significant part of the diet of the Sons of Light.

Interestingly, the ritual consumption of *Tirosh* ("new wine") is linked in the scrolls with the regular consumption of olive oil:

> *They are to consume the oil, from its special Feast Day to the Feast Day of New Oil—offered up on the altar—of the following year.*
> —TEMPLE SCROLL, col. 43:9–10

When contemporary researchers traveled to Crete to discover the secret of the incredible longevity of island residents, they concluded that their high consumption of olive oil correlates directly with a long and healthy life, marked by a remarkably low incidence of cardiopulmonary disease. The same may very well have been true of the Sons of Light.

Sabbath Delight

As discussed earlier, the Sons of Light understood well the concept of the Sabbath as an island in time, a restorative sanctuary wherein the soul is nourished and resuscitated. Food played a momentous role in actualizing this concept. An important passage from the community rule book (cited earlier in a different context) describes exactly how food was to be integrated into the Essenes' expression of Sabbath consciousness:

On the Sabbath day a person will only be allowed to eat
foods that have already been prepared in advance. No one is
to eat anything left out in the field. No one is to eat or drink
anything outside of the settlement.
—DAMASCUS RULE, col. 10:14–16, 22

The "sanctuary" of the rest day was not to be an excuse for labor of any sort, even in the preparation of food. The entire concept of living in a desert retreat is meaningless if the daily chore of food preparation is allowed to impinge on the one day when all labor must cease. This hardly meant that the Sons of Light were to fast on this, the weekly day of feasting! On the contrary, this day was to be a delight to the taste buds as well as to all the physical senses. If the whole of life were to be viewed as a banquet, how much more the Sabbath, which was meant to be a day of joy, not austerity. What then was the solution? It was simply that a double portion of Sabbath foods were to be prepared on Friday before sunset, sufficient for the covenantal community to dine all day Saturday as well as Friday night. The practice brings to mind the desert manna in the days of Moses' sojourn in the wilderness of Sinai:

Then the Lord said to Moses, "Behold, I will rain bread from
heaven for you; and the people shall go out and gather a day's
portion every day, that I may prove them, whether they will
walk in my law or not. On the sixth day, when they prepare
what they bring in, it will be twice as much as they gather daily."
—EXODUS 16:4–5

In the case of the Sons of Light, the double portion prepared on the eve of the Sabbath was to feed the Many, from sunset to sunset, from the coming in of the holy day to its bittersweet terminus, when darkness descended on Saturday.

Crime and Punishment, and the Sacred Meal

Since the consumption of food was conceived as a celebration of the holiness of life and the goodness of creation, the Essenes received a special requirement, that they go to a ritual immersion bath prior to the main meal of the day. This was in fact an ancient priestly ritual, also conducted at the great Temple in Jerusalem, when the priests would immerse themselves in a great bronze laver prior to conducting the sacrifice. For the members of this desert community, every individual had assumed a priestly role; everyone needed to obey the ancient rules regarding ritual immersion in water.

As for evildoers, there was hardly a greater punishment than to be excluded from the sacred meal. To be banned from the consecrated banquet was akin to excommunication. The rule book declares:

> *The unrighteous ones are not to immerse themselves in water—*
> *to be purified for partaking of the pure meal of the people of*
> *holiness. This is because they cannot be purified without first*
> *turning away from their evil deeds. Indeed, they are unclean,*
> *along with all who violate the divine word.*
>
> —MANUAL OF DISCIPLINE, col. 5:13–14

The rules also state:

> *If two witnesses should come forth—each one offering testimony*
> *regarding a different matter—the guilty one is to be banned from*
> *the pure Meal.*
>
> —DAMASCUS RULE, col. 9:20–21

It is further stressed that all members of the community were to pool their resources and their property in a common fund. Those who misrepresented the nature of their possessions were likewise excluded from the meal:

> *If a matter concerns material wealth, the testimony of two*
> *trustworthy witnesses is required—and the guilty person will*
> *be banned from the pure. A single witness is not accepted.*
> —DAMASCUS RULE, col. 9:22–23

Amazingly, proper behavior was regulated by something as simple as the right to sit with others in the great dining hall and the fear of losing that right. For even though the Sons of Light lived in splendid seclusion from the rest of humanity, they were by no means hermits. For humans, being social creatures by nature, the Essenes' philosophy was uncomplicated and basal. No one should live alone. No one should die alone. And certainly no one should dine alone. To take a meal in solitary isolation was an affront to God, who gave human beings each other. Therefore, partaking in the communal meal was a great impetus toward right conduct and toward repentance. Again, the rule book thunders:

> *Anyone at all, from among the people of the covenantal commu-*
> *nity—who deviously turns away from the commandments—will*
> *not be allowed to touch the pure Meal of the people of holiness.*
> *Such a person is not allowed to know about anything discussed*
> *in the community council, until his deeds are made clean from*
> *their iniquity—until he walks in the way of simple purity.*
> —MANUAL OF DISCIPLINE, col. 8:17–18

Priestly "Manna"

While all the Sons of Light were to treat themselves as though they were priests, engaging in certain ritual oblations, there was still a marked distinction between those who were lay members of the community and those who were born to the priestly class (members of the tribe of Levi). The longest of all the Secret Scrolls, the famous *Temple Scroll,* depicts a unique sort of consumption, a sacrificial feasting, which shall take place in some splendid future age, when a renewed priesthood shall officiate over the ceremonial slaughter of animals and subsequent consumption of copious quantities of meat, wine, and grain offerings:

> *On this day, all the heads of the tribes of Israel are to offer up to the Eternal—along with the wine—twelve rams.... These rams —along with grain offerings—will be offered according to the statute. Along with the drink offering, two tenths of the finest flour, mixed with oil, and one third of a hin of oil will be offered for each ram....*

> *They are to eat them before the Eternal One, in the outer courtyard. First, the priests are to drink; then, the Levites—the standard-bearers first ... and after them, all the people. From the greatest to the least, they will all drink the new wine. They will eat grapes as well, along with unripe fruits from the vines. For on this day, they will make atonement for the new wine.*
> —TEMPLE SCROLL, col. 19:15–16; 20:1–2; 21:3–8

Bear in mind, however, that no meal—not even the sacrifices offered in the Temple—was regarded as so "holy" that it couldn't be appreciated. Even the sacrifices prepared by the priests were not to be wasted but distributed among the Many. "They shall eat them on that day" is an important detail, not to be missed. There remains great misunderstanding, in the modern world as in antiquity, about what biblical "holiness" is. For example, the food from anyone's table was not to be set apart, or "reserved" for God (for some sacrificial purpose), so that it couldn't be enjoyed:

> No one is to devote to God the food of his own household, because it is written: "Each person hunts his brother with a net [or 'freewill offering': Micah 7:2]."
> —DAMASCUS RULE, col. 16:14–15

The word in Hebrew translated as "net" has a double meaning, signifying also a "devoted thing" such as a freewill offering to God.[28] In other words, if a Son of Light were to withhold food from his brother in need, claiming that it had been dedicated to God as a sacrifice, it was just as though he were hunting his brother with a net. For even sacrifices ("devoted things") were not to be thrown away and otherwise wasted but were to feed the congregation.

What about the gruesome and bloody nature of the sacrifices described? One hardly conceives of grain-based vegetarian fare, mixed with wild fowl and insects, given this and other elaborate descriptions of ritual slaughter in the *Temple Scroll*. Bear in mind, however, that this is a vision of the future, a golden messianic age, when the covenantal community shall preside, not from their desert refuge but from a rebuilt temple, standing proudly on Jerusalem's Mount Zion. At that time the Sons of Light had no temple from which to officiate. The Jerusalem Temple was out of bounds for their desert society, which visualized a day when they would be the ones performing the mandated sacrifices of the biblical text, not the corrupt priesthood in cahoots with the Romans, who at that time discharged the sacrificial service. Moreover, while the Bible mandates the sacrifice of animals, this wasn't the way the community lived at the moment.

For now, they were to offer a different kind of sacrifice, a sacrifice of praise, in a profusion of heartfelt prayers:

> *An offering of the lips—in accord with the holy ordinance—is like the pleasant fragrance of righteousness. It is like the simple perfection of the Way. It will be accepted as a freewill offering.*
> —MANUAL OF DISCIPLINE, col. 9:4–5

For now, they had to be content to live in the seclusion of the vast wasteland known as the Judean wilderness. For now they had to eat the manna of the wilderness: simple grains, fowl from the air, bats from the caves, and insects that creep upon the earth. It was simplicity turned to delicacy, transformed from the mundane to the guise of a great priestly banquet. This banquet was performed and enacted every day like a grand play upon the stage of eternity in the lives of every individual who became one of the Many.

10 Abundance:
Simple Perfection

EVERYTHING MATERIAL SOON *disappears in the substance of the whole; and everything causal is soon taken back into the universal reason; and the memory of everything is soon overwhelmed in time.*

Occupy thyself with few things, says the philosopher, if thou wouldst be tranquil .... For the greatest part of what we say and do being unnecessary, if a man takes this away, he will have more leisure and less uneasiness. Accordingly on every occasion a man should ask himself, Is this one of the unnecessary things?

—Marcus Aurelius, MEDITATIONS,
Book VII, 10; Book IV, 24

WHAT DOES A FOOL SEE? A PERSON'S *clothes. What does the wise one see? A person's spirit.*

—THE ZOHAR

YOU CANNOT SERVE GOD AND MAMMON.

—Jesus, LUKE 16:13

MAMMON" is a biblical term (Aramaic in origin) that generally refers to all things material, all corporeal substance. It has to do with one's possessions, one's property and equity, and, most importantly, one's attitude toward all things owned. An important measure of any individual is the way in which that person views the material world around him or her. Obviously, the array of personal possessions, which enhance and occasionally crowd our lives, is boundless. People define themselves by what they own. Success is most often defined in material terms. In contrast, the spiritually sensitive Sons of Light were dedicated to freeing the individual from the slavish pursuit of mammon.

Those who had come to this splendid little utopia, nestled in one corner of the vast Judean wilderness, had fundamentally redefined their relation to the material. However it may seem at first glance, they did not deny themselves whatever amenities their age might provide. Their spartan tastes reflected not some rigid self-denial, but a simplicity of lifestyle that found joy in the bonds of love, peace in boundless compassion for all Sons of Light, and eternal awe in nature's great pageant. The things so valued by other people and other societies, for which they struggle and strive and seek all the days of their lives, seemed trivial to the Sons of Light. In the brilliance of the night sky, in the restless desert streams, in the great stretches of the burning sand, in the lonely cliffs that dominate the horizon to the west they had glimpsed this bold injunction: Be not enamored of the things of this world. They had also read it in the rule book of the Many:

> *They are to keep themselves separate from the sons of the pit.*
> *They are to stay far away from the material wealth of wicked-*
> *ness. It is unclean, having been gained through a rash vow,*
> *through that which is banned, or even from the treasury of the*

> *temple. They are not to steal from the poor among the people,*
> *making widows of their victims and murdering orphans.*
> —DAMASCUS RULE, col. 6:15–17

There was no better exemplar of avarice, according to the Secret Scrolls, than the Jerusalemite priesthood. These presumed shepherds of the flock had grown fat from tithes and offerings, from money "vowed" to sacred use, which they had amassed in enormous quantity for themselves. Of one character in particular, a shadowy figure called the "Wicked Priest," it was said:

> *He stole and stockpiled the material wealth of the people of vio-*
> *lence—the ones who had rebelled against the Eternal. He also*
> *took away the material wealth of the people, adding to his litany*
> *of evil.*
> —HABAKKUK COMMENTARY, col. 8:11–12

When widows go hungry, when the fatherless are uncared for, when want and extremity are experienced by any of God's children, the clear responsibility of those who have is to share with those who have not. But this was not how the priests behaved, nor was it how anyone in particular behaved in the world "out there." That was why the Sons of Light built an alternate society, an exemplary fraternity, where munificence ruled the day. Regarding their personal conduct, the ancient historian notes the requirements enjoined upon each one of the Many:

> *... that he will keep his hands clear from theft, and his soul*
> *from unlawful gains; and that he will neither conceal any-*
> *thing from those of his own sect, nor discover any of their*
> *doctrines to others, no, not though any one should compel*
> *him so to do at the hazard of his life.*
> —Josephus, WARS, II, VIII, 7

Again, it is written:

... that he will abstain from robbery, and will equally pre-
serve the books belonging to their sect, and the names of the
angels [or messengers.] These are the oaths by which they
secure their proselytes to themselves.
—Josephus, WARS, II, VIII, 7

It is insightful that abstaining from robbery is made equivalent to the holy task of "preserving the books." There is a powerful linkage here between the Essenes' attitude toward the
material world—being unmotivated by the desire to steal—and
copying the sacred writings, thereby becoming stewards of the
divine Word. The reason is profoundly uncomplicated. The Sons
of Light were pedagogues of the people, and in refraining from
avarice as well as in preserving the sacred books, they were
transmitting the wisdom of the ages by which this distinctly nonmaterial "Way" was made known. They taught by example.
Their example was the greatest preceptor of all, and through
them the whole world would someday learn the Way of truth.

The Way and the Tao

The Teacher of Righteousness had spoken—in a manner
not unlike the great sage of Taoism, Lao-tzu—and made clear
the Way. One must jettison all restive struggling for material
bounty and property. The Way (like the Tao) consists of finding
harmony with life's great patterns, not of striving to attain, to
acquire, or to advance the self. Live openly, transparently,
without machinations and stratagems designed to "get ahead."
For the last shall be first and the first shall be last. This is the
Way of perfection. The community rule book describes both
those who turn aside from the Way, and those who have chosen to walk in it:

Whoever decides not to belong to the Covenant of the Eternal—
in order to persist in the obstinance of his own heart—will not
ever be allowed to come into the Community of Truth.... His
knowledge, his energy, and his material wealth will not be
brought into the Council of the Community. This is because he
plows the mud of evil. By the time he returns, he is defiled.
—MANUAL OF DISCIPLINE, col. 2:25–26; 3:2–3

With regard to the material wealth of the people of holiness....
Those who walk in simple perfection are not to mix their own
material wealth with the material wealth of deceivers—for they
have not purified their way; nor have they separated themselves
from wickedness or walked in the Way of simple perfection.
—MANUAL OF DISCIPLINE, col. 9:8–9

The references to "possessions" and to "property" refer to
all corporeal things, the injunction being quite simply to resist
the materialism of the general culture. The Sons of Light were
to retreat with those of like mind to a society not dominated by
the naked aggressiveness of people who pursue the mammon
of unrighteousness. They were to rise above the craving for
wealth and the ardor for affluence. They were to replace lust
for things and "thinginess" with personal *nothingness*. They
were to be like hollow reeds, devoid of earthly desires within
but erect and sturdy without. The quality of life they sought is
expressed in the ancient hymnody of the Many:

I will never let a wicked spirit make me envious of anyone. I will
never let my soul lust after material wealth gained by force.
—MANUAL OF DISCIPLINE, col. 10:18–19

It isn't just booty captured in war that is proscribed but
also the relentless and solicitous pursuit of wealth, which is just
as much an act of aggression. Whereas envy involves the desire

for things external to the self, the Way counsels being content inside one's own skin, developing one's sense of self-worth, and finding the repose of the soul. When it comes to materialism and the pursuit of wealth, the Sons of Light (like the Eastern sage Lao-tzu) declared that the most efficacious possible action is inaction. Thoreau said with typical aplomb: "A man is rich in proportion to the things he can afford to let alone." Among the Sons of Light, the greater part of all that is material could indeed be let alone, and to this extent they were wealthy beyond speaking. The ancient historian describes the community with flair and passion:

> *These men are despisers of riches, and so very communicative as raises our admiration. Nor is there any one to be found among them who hath more than another; for it is a law among them, that those who come to them must let what they have be common to the whole order, inasmuch, that among them all there is no appearance of poverty or excess of riches, but every one's possessions are intermingled with every other's possessions; and so there is, as it were, one patrimony among all the brethren.*
> —Josephus, WARS, II, VIII, 3

"Despisers of riches" doesn't mean a hatred for money, no matter how the passage sounds at first glance. It means that these were people who had divested themselves of personal fortune, contributing all they owned to the common fund, thereby calling nothing their own. The community rule book lays out the procedures whereby all new members were admitted into the commonwealth:

> *If it should be a person's good fortune to come into the community's secret council . . . all of his material wealth and all of his earnings will be turned over to the Overseer of the earnings of*

*the Many. It will be credited to the Overseer's account and will
not be used for the Many....*

*When a second year has passed ... if it is determined that his des-
tiny is to become a full member of the Community ... all of his
material wealth will be merged with the community.*
—Manual of Discipline, col. 6:18–22

Unlike the rest of society, where money has always been
what matters most, the Sons of Light had no rigid social caste
system based on wealth. But this does not imply a lack of order.
Rank among the Many was instead a function of a person's
knowledge, coupled with his seniority as a member of the community. Designated individuals of mature constitution called
"stewards" were appointed to oversee the proper distribution
of all things material. Poverty, hunger, and want were therefore
nonexistent, having been replaced by a single interdependent
commonwealth—a "patrimony"—linking each one with his
fellow. The ancient historian writes:

*They also have stewards appointed to take care of their common
affairs, who every one of them have no separate business for any,
but what is for the use of them all.*
—Josephus, WARS, II, VIII, 3

"No separate business" means a merging of enterprise, a
union of industry, resulting in a completely shared material culture. The Secret Scrolls expound it thus:

*Every time one person is found in the company of another, the
comrade of lower rank is to submit to the comrade of higher
rank. This pertains to anything related to work or to material
possessions (mammon). Together they will dine. Together they*

will offer blessings. Together they will make their deliberations.
—MANUAL OF DISCIPLINE, col. 6:2–3

Elsewhere the historian writes:

And truly, as for other things, they do nothing but according to the injunctions of their curators; only these two things are done among them at every one's own free will, which are, to assist those that want it, and to show mercy; for they are permitted of their own accord to afford succor to such as deserve it, when they stand in need of it, and to bestow food on those that are in distress; but they cannot give anything to their kindred without the curators.
—Josephus, WARS, II, VIII, 6

The altruistic ethic the Essenes conveyed, accruing to the common good, was served by each Son of Light giving according to his ability, each one receiving according to his need. Again the historian writes:

This is demonstrated by that institution of theirs, which will not suffer anything to hinder them from having all things in common; so that a rich man enjoys no more of his own wealth than he who hath nothing at all.
—Josephus, ANTIQUITIES, XVIII, I, 5

Yes, the Essenes had a hierarchy, but it was a hierarchy of knowledge and wisdom that bound them together as they traversed the self-revealing Way. It wasn't a moneyed hierarchy. To the contrary, on a material level it was a complete social leveling, quite remarkable in an age of slaves and masters, of impoverished serfs laboring under back-breaking conditions to improve the lot of lords and landowners. The Sons of Light, however, were secure in their desert hideaway, not to be threatened by the malevolent and swirling currents without, not to be devoured by the carnivorous humanoid beasts who ruled and reigned across the land to the west. As long as the community was left alone, they would be serenely independent, beholden to no one, living out their years in unmolested harmony.

Simple Abundance

There is a widely held misconception that spirituality means renunciation, self-denial, and asceticism and that seeking spiritual resonance in life necessarily involves giving up a multitude of creature comforts, which are generally replaced by sackcloth and ashes. Not so for the Sons of Light. As for the physical engineering of their settlement, it was nothing short of a marvel. While the Many continued to reside in the caves that pockmarked the limestone cliffs to the west, the plaster-covered communal buildings, including an imposing central tower, shimmered in the effulgent sunshine. There were ornate stone pillars of finely carved, fluted elegance. There was a marvelously engineered aqueduct for water which coursed from the distant hills directly into the settlement, where it linked the communal buildings. The precious liquid was funneled into a series of finely plastered cisterns and ritual immersion baths (*mikvaot*), providing more than ample water all year round. There were stables for beasts of burden, a laundry for the cleansing of garments, and an enormous pantry, where hundreds of dishes were architecturally stacked. A kiln on-site fired an abundance of pottery, which was capable of storing a plentiful amount of foodstuffs.

They may have lived in splendid isolation, but isolation did not mean quarantine. They may have been sheltered and sequestered, but they had not been cut off. Trade was still conducted with the outside, and all manner of material commodities, not produced on-site, were brought in from other parts. For example, there was exquisite glassware on hand, imported from across the sea. Various oils, spices, and libations had also been brought in, insuring that their lifestyle was lacking in nothing. Anyone who happened to survey the artificially created oasis in the desert was aware instantly that those who lived here, far from being a caste of eccentric hermits, lived a quality of life superior to that of the nations round about.

But what brought about such a level of prosperity? It is widely observed that the wealthiest people of any era tend also to be the most frugal, who waste the least, who save the most, who abide by the elemental principles of thrift, economy, and temperance. The formula is irrefutable: frugality plus time equals wealth.

Frugality plus consistency is the key. Frugality does not equal asceticism. It does, however, equal conservation. Thoreau perhaps said it best: "Beware of all enterprises that require new clothes." The Sons of Light seem to have invented this admonition, as witnessed by the historian:

> *Nor do they allow of the change of garments, or of shoes, till they be first entirely torn to pieces, or worn out by time. Nor do they either buy or sell anything to one another; but every one of them gives what he hath to him that wanteth it, and receives from him again in lieu of it what may be convenient for himself; and although there be no requital made, they are fully allowed to take what they want of whomsoever they please.*
> —Josephus, WARS, II, VIII, 4

Make no mistake, the desire for things new is one of the perennial destroyers of accumulated wealth. Instead of continuing to use things that are still usable, most people would rather have something new, even if acquiring that new thing entails an unusual degree of indebtedness. The best advice for individuals is also the first principle among the Many:

> It matters not how much you make; the only thing that matters is how much you save.

A case in point is the way in which the headquarters settlement, located on the shore of Lake Asphaltis, was linked with other colonies of Essenes across Judea. While the desert encampment was the locus of organization for the entire movement, there was in fact a "commonwealth," a complete material union that amalgamated them with their comrades, wherever covenantal communities had been planted. The cooperatives communicated with one another through a series of emissaries who traveled the countryside of greater Judea with great dispatch, bringing guidance and direction from the wilderness headquarters. There is no clearer illustration of the attitude of the Sons of Light toward material life than the way in which these emissaries behaved. Since there was a complete monetary and fiduciary union among the Many, there was simply no need to take any specie along with them. The ancient historian testifies accordingly:

> For which reason they carry nothing with them when they travel into remote parts, though still they take their weapons with them, for fear of thieves. Accordingly there is, in every city where they live, one appointed particularly to take care of strangers, and provide garments and other necessaries for them.
> —Josephus, WARS, II, VIII, 4

Again, we have the idea of "stewards," individuals specifically given charge of distributing the general bounty to those in need—in this case, to traveling emissaries but in a broader sense to any who merit the status of "strangers."

Never were the Sons of Light to be found wanting. The pattern was one of simple abundance:

> *Intone blessings, oh my soul! Intone blessings for all the wonders of the Eternal. May the divine Name be blessed; for the Eternal has rescued the soul of the "poor" and has never scorned those who are humble.... The Eternal has transformed their darkness into bright light and turned their winding pathways into a level plain. The Eternal has bestowed upon them the ways of peace and truth.... They have also been given a completely different heart, so that they may walk ... in the way of the divine heart.*
> —BLESS, OH MY SOUL (4Q434), frag. 1, col. 1:1–2, 9–11

Poor of the Spirit

The irony of it all is that by virtue of the extraordinary assets that accumulated in Essene treasuries for nearly two centuries, they were rich beyond imagining. There was gold. There was silver. There were gemstones. There was copious coinage. All of this belonged to the Many. Yet, they were also penniless, owning nothing personally, quintessentially "poor." A term was devised to describe this startling irony, a term that crept its way into the Secret Scrolls. Among a number of other designations describing the Sons of Light, they were also known as the "poor of the spirit."

It is an appellation conveniently borrowed by Jesus of Nazareth, with a slight twist:

> *Blessed are the poor in spirit, for theirs is the kingdom of heaven.*
> —MATTHEW 5:3

The common idea about this famous passage is that Jesus, who was, after all, a Jewish sage in his own right, is commending those who are "spiritually poor," down on their luck, as it were, promising them a heavenly reward in the world to come. The Secret Scrolls, however, reveal the original context of the term. The reference is not at all to spiritual poverty, for the phrase ought to be translated "poor of the spirit," connoting those who (by virtue of having pooled their resources) are officially "poor" but who do in fact possess the spirit. It refers to those who are—by virtue of having relinquished material property and ungainly possessions that hinder (rather than enhance) spiritual resonance—powerful and mighty in a purely metaphysical sense.

For those who belonged to the Many, there was no question about what the meaning of this locution was. The great *War Scroll,* which describes a series of apocalyptic conflicts to be fought at the end of the age, uses the term in the precise manner intended:

> *Through the poor of the spirit, there is dominion over all the hardhearted ones. Through the perfect of the Way, all the nations of wickedness will be obliterated. None of their "heroes" can stand any longer. We, however, are the true remnant of Your people.*
> —WAR SCROLL, col. 14:7–8

From the mysterious *Psalms Scroll* we find another reference to the paradoxical might of the "poor":

> *You have done wondrous things with the one who is "poor"—in order to reveal Your greatness through me, to all the sons of Adam.*
> —PSALMS SCROLL, col. 13:15–16

The real message of both the *War Scroll* and the *Psalms Scroll,* all presumed militancy notwithstanding, is that humility and contrition, coupled with a nonmaterial view of the universe, shall win the day and triumph over brute force of nations, which value a material orientation over all. In God's economy human principles are reversed, mortal wisdom controverted. Paradox is the key. The poor are rich and the rich are poor. The last are first and the first last.

Bear in mind, however, that only in the context of a committed community can such irony find genuine expression. If one seeks to be "poor" individually so as not to be miserly, one becomes a hermit. But if one shares one's bounty with family members or with a larger community, one becomes, like the ancient Sons of Light, richly poor and poorly rich. The payoff is in power and in spirit. The Son of Light was relieved of the burdensome notion that he must produce, that he must sell, that he must accumulate riches in order to live a certain way. The pressure was off. The individual was to labor for the joy—yes, joy—of labor, of which the prosperity of the whole community (and the individual Son of Light with it) was a natural and inexorable by-product.

Treasure!

The frugal lifestyle adopted by the Many translated into a very great surplus, an abundance of material wealth that, as noted, wasn't experienced as personal wealth by any among them. This wealth was a direct by-product of desert thrift, the inescapable result of lives lived in unison and harmony and dedicated to a common purpose. Attitudes toward wealth produce, therefore, a unique paradox; for the great wealth of the community is owned, at the very same time, by everyone and by no one. The Many were wealthy beyond imagining, yet utterly poor.

There is one scroll in particular, fashioned of a very high grade of copper, upon which the contents of a vast treasury of accumulated wealth were inscribed. It is without question one of the largest inventories of buried treasure (some two hundred tons of silver and gold) ever recorded in human history. This single artifact tells us, in all likelihood, what the Sons of Light managed to save and sequester during the twenty-odd decades of their existence. To call this register impressive would be a monumental understatement, for included in the list, among other items, are:

- a crate full of silver, with a total weight of seventeen talents[29]
- one hundred bars of gold
- nine hundred talents
- forty talents of silver
- sixty-five bars of gold
- six hundred pitchers of silver
- gold and silver vessels to be used for the tithe ... six hundred nine, all together
- thirteen plus talents
- two hundred talents of silver
- seventy talents of silver
- tithe vessels, including coins bearing figures
- thirty-two talents
- forty-two talents
- nine talents
- four hundred talents
- eighty talents of gold, inside two pitchers
- seventeen talents of silver and gold
- seventy talents of silver
- twenty-two talents
- silver from the sanctified offerings

- three hundred talents of gold
- eighty talents
- forty talents
- a crate, with all manner of vessels, and sixty talents of silver

Moreover, the explicit whereabouts of the treasure are delineated. The locations, scattered across the Judean wilderness, range from Jericho to Jerusalem, including a famous ancient tomb located to the immediate east of Jerusalem, in the Kidron Valley, called Absalom's Pillar.

The *Copper Scroll* became an instant sensation when a team of archaeologists discovered it in a cave near Qumran in 1952. In spite of the precision of the treasure locations, not a trace of the cache has ever been recovered, and the scroll has generated many more questions than it has answered. Is the treasure real or fictive? Is it the treasure of the Essenes, or perhaps the contents of the Temple treasury, taken from Jerusalem and buried across the wilderness for safekeeping?[30] Some think it represents monies collected not by the Essenes but by later rabbinic authorities long after the Temple was destroyed, for its eventual rebuilding. The most responsible position remains, however, that the *Copper Scroll* describes a real treasure accumulated by the desert cooperative over the two centuries of their existence.

How were the Sons of Light able to amass such staggering amounts of treasure? Trade, no doubt, accounts for the bulk of it. The settlement was located along one of the most prosperous trade routes to the east—toward Moab, Edom, and Nabatea. A mixture of salts, spices, and exotic oils from the vicinity of Lake Asphaltis were of great value in those days, even as products from the Dead Sea remain lucrative some twenty centuries later. Add to the profits of trade the revenues brought into the community by new members, all of whom divested themselves of their worldly belongings upon joining themselves to the Many, and a substantial reserve could easily be created.

All in all, we have in the *Copper Scroll* a stunning verification of the community's attitude toward material wealth, proving that a lifestyle of frugality may yield incredible recompense.

The Kibbutz

The direct descendant of the community of the Sons of Light may well be the contemporary farming settlement that forms the backbone of modern Israeli agriculture, the "kibbutz." The word means "collective," and that it truly is. In today's kibbutz system (consisting of roughly 270 agricultural collectives scattered across Israel), all things are held in common, from personal finances to the land itself. Families live together, children are raised together, young people dorm together. Individually, no one owns anything, but collectively, the kibbutzim have traditionally been one of the wealthiest and most influential sectors of Israeli society. Many individual kibbutzim are quite affluent, possessing every imaginable modern amenity. While farming remains the hallmark of the kibbutz, most also engage in some form of manufacturing and light industry. All are wealthy, yet all are poor. Theft is nonexistent. There are no locks on doors. Each contributes according to his or her ability; each receives according to his or her need. Call it communist, call it socialist, call it whatever you like, but the fact is, it works.

Some of the greatest and most influential leaders of modern Israel are in fact products of the kibbutz system, including

Golda Meir, who emigrated from Milwaukee to join an Israeli agricultural cooperative. On the kibbutz she acquired the leadership traits that would later serve her at the helm of Israel's government. There was also David Ben-Gurion, Israel's first prime minister, who never lost his "desert vision," no matter what direction his professional and political career took him. Like the ancient Sons of Light, he was obsessed by a form of messianism, seeking to transmit to the whole nation a messianic burden, that it might become an "exemplary state." The state of Israel's future, he declared, is to be found not in crowded municipalities but in the desert! While there are kibbutzim scattered across the length and breadth of Israel, it was in this desert kibbutz that Ben-Gurion felt most at home. There he lived, with his wife, to a ripe old age, laboring on the land yet surrounded by his many books, doubtless cultivating the same disciplines developed so long ago by the ancient sect on the shore of the Dead Sea.

The Israeli kibbutz remains a model for communal living, untainted by greed and materialism. Today, more than two millennia later, it is very much akin to the ancient desert society perched on the edge of eternity, and speaking from their age to ours.

Shangri-La

What is the legacy of this long-lost fraternity, whose sacred parchments have resurfaced after so long an entombment? What principles of theirs can we imbibe, apply to today, and make our own?

Certainly the idea of a community that has banished materialism and the lust for possessions brings to mind the many visions of utopian societies that have been formulated down through time. One cannot but recall a most remarkable novel that captivated the hearts of millions of readers during some of the darkest and most difficult days of the twentieth century. James Hilton's *Lost Horizon* provided Western culture with a visionary glimpse into a society few had ever dreamed of. Just as Thomas More coined a term for an ideal fraternity— "Utopia"—that filtered into the language itself, so *Lost Horizon* spawned a single word—Shangri-La—that inspired multitudes in the grip of the Great Depression. Published in 1933, *Lost Horizon* tells the fanciful story of four passengers on a hijacked airplane who are whisked away to a high and lofty, uncharted territory, beyond a stunning mountain range, "... floating, in appearance, upon vast levels of cloud."

After crash-landing in a remote region of Tibet, the dazed passengers discover that they are in reasonable proximity to a most amazing settlement, a utopian community called Shangri-La. It is sufficiently isolated so that the rest of humankind is unaware of its existence. Yet this "Lost Horizon" is hardly primitive. It contains the most modern amenities, including plumbing made in Akron, Ohio. The amazing "Valley of the Blue Moon," nestled deep among the mountain ranges, is well suited to agriculture, and every available inch is cultivated. It is a small society of between one thousand and fifteen hundred souls, who labor equally, with no servitude and no regard for rank and position. The community is governed by a High Lama, a religious leader who rules not as a despot, but in coordination with other lamas. It is a theocracy, but a wise and tolerant theocracy.

Moreover, it is a society devoid of class distinctions, without the domination of any single individual over anyone else. As for material culture, people's homes are unassuming, as is their manner of attire. The inhabitants do not bejewel themselves with baubles and trinkets but dress in attractive, though modest and functional, apparel. Gold is to be found in copious quantity in the nearby Valley of the Blue Moon, but none covet it, since the accumulation of personal wealth is of no interest to anyone. The yellow metal is simply used for trade, in payment for needed items imported from the outside.

Shangri-La doesn't exist in a self-sufficient vacuum. It recognizes the existence of the world beyond, but its people have made a simple decision not to be ravaged by it. The whole of human culture is to be studied and learned from, and education devotes itself to this purpose. Any subject may be taken up in great detail, from literature to science to linguistics. Life in all of its wonders is to be enjoyed. Pleasure is freely undertaken, including the joy of eating, drinking, and sexuality.

But delectation is balanced by an overarching principle: moderation in all things. The end result is an extension of the human life cycle, whereby individuals, liberated from the corruption that can devour one's days like a rootless phantom, live to be incredibly advanced in years. Worry, anxiety, and apprehension are replaced by meditation and the contemplative quest for the essence of life. The same moderation controls romantic behavior, resulting in lasting marriages and the complete absence of divorce. As for spiritual values, Shangri-La embraces a variety of faiths, from Taoism to Confucianism to Buddhism, with their attendant shrines standing alongside each other in symbiotic relationship. No single religion has a monopoly on truth. Therefore no religion is entirely correct; neither is any religion entirely incorrect. Every human faith is "moderately true."

All citizens of Shangri-La are treated with justice and egalitarian respect. Neither laws nor law enforcement officers are required, since the root causes of dissension have been removed. Instead, the community's existence is predicated on a common idea that integrates the society—that global war is inevitable, that a terrible cataclysm is destined to destroy human civilization, that a place of refuge is required, the peculiar destiny of which is to preserve the accumulated knowledge of the species. Shangri-La's particular raison d'être is to gather and collect the ideas, the art, the music, and the important books of the world in a kind of repository, so that all the merit, worth, and originality of humankind will not be lost forever.

James Hilton wrote his masterpiece fifteen years before the Dead Sea Scrolls mysteriously surfaced. But the utopian resonance of the Secret Scrolls is familiar to us. Amazingly the ancient Judeans of two millennia ago developed their own ideal society, in a place almost as secluded as the mountains of Tibet. They also feared a great cataclysmic war, and the egalitarian society they founded was, in their day and age, equally a treasure trove of wisdom and knowledge, reproduced in the most remarkable hidden library in human history.

Every one of us is drawn to the dream of an ideal place, a paradise on earth where wealth, ego, and domination are replaced by equality, toleration, compassion, and spiritual simplicity. The community of Qumran seems to have been such a place. The records the Sons of Light left behind offer us their wisdom for creating some vestige of this simplicity—and consequent abundance—in our own lives.

1 This and subsequent quotations from Marcus Aurelius are taken from *The Meditations of Marcus Aurelius,* trans. George Long (London: Collins Clear-Type Press, 1957).

2 In Hebrew they are called *ha-megilot ha-genozut* (המגילות הגנוזות), or "Hidden Scrolls." They were not only hidden, but secreted away for two millennia, and I have therefore adopted this nomenclature.

3 Author's translation.

4 Martin Buber, *I and Thou,* trans. Walter Kaufmann (New York: Charles Scribner's Sons, 1970), p. 62.

5 The bulk of chimpanzee observation in the wild has been done by the Englishwoman Jane Goodall and her earlier counterpart in the world of mountain gorillas, Dian Fossey.

6 "The Many" (הרבים) is a term used repeatedly in the Dead Sea Scrolls to describe the essential harmony experienced by a community of close-knit souls, bound by sacred covenant.

7 The location is known today by the Arabic nomenclature "Qumran," meaning "dome," because of the shape of the cliffs to the immediate west.

8 See the *Damascus Rule,* col. 10:6.

9 See Edward M. Hallowell, M.D., *Connect* (New York: Pantheon Books, 1999).

10 See Deuteronomy 6:4, the central declaration of Judaism: "Hear O Israel, the Lord our God, the Lord is One (*Ekhad*)!"

11 See George Brown Tindall, *America: A Narrative History,* vol. 1, 2d ed. (New York: W. W. Norton & Company, 1988), pp. 526–529.

12 See Chaim Potok, *Wanderings* (New York: Fawcett Crest, 1978), p. 502–503.

13 Ibid., p. 502.

14 See Ziauddin Sardar, *Muhammad* (Cambridge, England: Icon Books, 1994).

15 Abraham Joshua Heschel, *The Sabbath* (New York: Farrah, Straus, and Giroux, 1951), p. 5.

16 Ibid., pp. 5–6.

17 See *The Quotable Einstein*, ed. Alice Calaprise (Princeton, NJ: Princeton University Press, 1996), p. 234.

18 Ibid., p. 214.

19 As Magen Broshi, curator emeritus of the Shrine of the Book, has stated, "One of the reasons they went to the desert was to prepare themselves for that kind of war."

20 Talmud, *Berachot* 63.

21 See Hirsch Lieb Gordon, "The Musar Yeshivah: A Memoir," in Paul Mendes-Flohr and Yehuda Reinharz, eds., *The Jew in the Modern World* (New York: Oxford University Press, 1995), p. 396.

22 Patrick Glynn, *God: The Evidence—The Reconciliation of Faith and Reason in a Postsecular World* (Rocklin, CA: Prima Publishing, 1999), p. 9.

23 *The Quotable Einstein*, p. 97.

24 Quoted in Sarah Ban Breathnach, *Simple Abundance,* s.v. August 9 (New York: Warner Books, 1995).

25 *Manual of Discipline*, col. 3:7.

26 *Manual of Discipline*, col. 4:9, 11.

27 The actual passage reads: "nor by *alef* and *lamed* [אל i.e., *Elohim*— "God"] or by *alef* and *dalet* [אד i.e., *Adonai*—"Lord"]. . . ."

28 Students of Hebrew will be interested to note the precise word used here: *Herem* (חרם).

29 A talent is a measure of weight, the rough equivalent of seventy-five pounds or thirty-four kilograms. The bulleted items come from various passages of the *Copper Scroll*.

30 Bear in mind that the land of Israel was systematically pillaged by the Romans from the year 66 to 70 of the Common Era, in response to a massive revolt launched by the independence-minded Zealot faction.